Samuel Langhorne Clemens (November 30, 1835 – April 21, 1910), known by his pen name Mark Twain, was an American writer, humorist, entrepreneur, publisher, and lecturer. He was lauded as the "greatest humorist this country has produced", and William Faulkner called him "the father of American literature". His novels include The Adventures of Tom Sawyer (1876) and its sequel, the Adventures of Huckleberry Finn (1884), the latter often called "The Great American Novel".

Twain was raised in Hannibal, Missouri, which later provided the setting for Tom Sawyer and Huckleberry Finn. He served an apprenticeship with a printer and then worked as a typesetter, contributing articles to the newspaper of his older brother Orion Clemens. He later became a riverboat pilot on the Mississippi River before heading west to join Orion in Nevada. (Source: Wikipedia)

Literary works:

The Gilded Age: A Tale of Today (1873)
The Prince and the Pauper (1881)
A Connecticut Yankee in
King Arthur's Court (1889)
The American Claimant (1892)
Pudd'nhead Wilson (1894)
Personal Recollections of Joan of Arc (1896)
A Horse's Tale (1907)
The Mysterious Stranger (1916, posthumous)
The Adventures of Tom Sawyer (1876)
Adventures of Huckleberry Finn (1884)
Tom Sawyer Abroad (1894)
Tom Sawyer, Detective (1896)
"Eve's Diary" (1906)

MARK TWAIN'S LETTERS

VOLUME 5 & 6

MARK TWAIN

PRINCE CLASSICS

PRINCE CLASSICS

First Printing: 2020

ISBN 978-93-5385-546-8 (paperback)

ISBN 978-93-5385-547-5 (Hardcover)

Published by Prince Classics

www.princeclassics.com

Contents

MARK TWAIN'S LETTERS
VOLUME 5 & 6

MARK TWAIN'S LETTERS—1853-1866

VOLUME 5

XL. LETTERS OF 1901, CHIEFLY TO TWICHELL. MARK TWAIN AS A REFORMER. SUMMER AT SARANAC. ASSASSINATION OF PRESIDENT McKINLEY.

An editorial in the Louisville Courier-Journal, early in 1901, said: "A remarkable transformation, or rather a development, has taken place in Mark Twain. The genial humorist of the earlier day is now a reformer of the vigorous kind, a sort of knight errant who does not hesitate to break a lance with either Church or State if he thinks them interposing on that broad highway over which he believes not a part but the whole of mankind has the privilege of passing in the onward march of the ages."

Mark Twain had begun "breaking the lance" very soon after his return from Europe. He did not believe that he could reform the world, but at least he need not withhold his protest against those things which stirred his wrath. He began by causing the arrest of a cabman who had not only overcharged but insulted him; he continued by writing openly against the American policy in the Philippines, the missionary propaganda which had resulted in the Chinese uprising and massacre, and against Tammany politics. Not all of his efforts were in the line of reform; he had become a sort of general spokesman which the public flocked to hear, whatever the subject. On the occasion of a Lincoln Birthday service at Carnegie Hall he was chosen to preside, and he was obliged to attend more dinners than were good for his health. His letters of this period were mainly written to his old friend Twichell, in Hartford. Howells, who lived in New York, he saw with considerable frequency.

In the letter which follows the medicine which Twichell was to take was Plasmon, an English proprietary remedy in which Mark Twain had invested—a panacea for all human ills which osteopathy could not reach.

To Rev. Joseph Twichell, in Hartford:

14 W. 10TH ST. Jan. 23, '01.

DEAR JOE,—Certainly. I used to take it in my coffee, but it settled to the bottom in the form of mud, and I had to eat it with a spoon; so I dropped the custom and took my 2 teaspoonfuls in cold milk after breakfast. If we were out of milk I shoveled the dry powder into my mouth and washed it down with water. The only essential is to get it down, the method is not important.

No, blame it, I can't go to the Alumni dinner, Joe. It takes two days, and I can't spare the time. Moreover I preside at the Lincoln birthday celebration in Carnegie Hall Feb. 11, and I must not make two speeches so close together. Think of it—two old rebels functioning there—I as President, and Watterson as Orator of the Day! Things have changed somewhat in these 40 years, thank God.

Look here—when you come down you must be our guest—we've got a roomy room for you, and Livy will make trouble if you go elsewhere. Come straight to 14 West 10th.

Jan. 24. Livy says Amen to that; also, can you give us a day or two's notice, so the room will be sure to be vacant?

I'm going to stick close to my desk for a month, now, hoping to write a small book.

Ys Ever

MARK

The letter which follows is a fair sample of Mark Twain's private violence on a subject which, in public print, he could only treat effectively by preserving his good humor. When he found it necessary to boil over, as he did, now and then, for relief, he always found a willing audience in Twichell. The mention of his "Private Philosophy" refers to 'What Is Man?', privately published in 1906; reissued by his publishers in 1916.

To Rev. J. H. Twichell, in Hartford:

14 W. 10th Jan. 29, '01.

DEAR JOE,—I'm not expecting anything but kicks for scoffing, and am expecting a diminution of my bread and butter by it, but if Livy will let me I will have my say. This nation is like all the others that have been spewed upon the earth—ready to shout for any cause that will tickle its vanity or fill its pocket. What a hell of a heaven it will be, when they get all these hypocrites assembled there!

I can't understand it! You are a public guide and teacher, Joe, and are under a heavy responsibility to men, young and old; if you teach your people—as you teach me—to hide their opinions when they believe the flag is being abused and dishonored, lest the utterance do them and a publisher a damage, how do you answer for it to your conscience? You are sorry for me; in the fair way of give and take, I am willing to be a little sorry for you.

However, I seem to be going counter to my own Private Philosophy—which Livy won't allow me to publish—because it would destroy me. But I hope to see it in print before I die. I planned it 15 years ago, and wrote it in '98. I've often tried to read it to Livy, but she won't have it; it makes her melancholy. The truth always has that effect on people. Would have, anyway, if they ever got hold of a rag of it—Which they don't.

You are supposing that I am supposing that I am moved by a Large Patriotism, and that I am distressed because our President has blundered up to his neck in the Philippine mess; and that I am grieved because this great big ignorant nation, which doesn't know even the A B C facts of the Philippine episode, is in disgrace before the sarcastic world—drop that idea! I care nothing for the rest—I am only distressed and troubled because I am befouled by these things. That is all. When I search myself away down deep, I find this out. Whatever a man feels or thinks or does, there is never any but one reason for it—and that is a selfish one.

At great inconvenience, and expense of precious time I went to the chief synagogue the other night and talked in the interest of a charity school of poor Jew girls. I know—to the finest, shades—the selfish ends that moved me; but no one else suspects. I could give you the details if I had time. You would perceive how true they are.

I've written another article; you better hurry down and help Livy squelch it.

She's out pottering around somewhere, poor housekeeping slave; and Clara is in the hands of the osteopath, getting the bronchitis pulled and hauled out of her. It was a bad attack, and a little disquieting. It came day before yesterday, and she hasn't sat up till this afternoon. She is getting along satisfactorily, now.

Lots of love to you all.

MARK

Mark Twain's religion had to do chiefly with humanity in its present incarnation, and concerned itself very little with any possible measure of reward or punishment in some supposed court of the hereafter. Nevertheless, psychic investigation always interested him, and he was good-naturedly willing to explore, even hoping, perhaps, to be convinced that individuality continues beyond death. The letter which follows indicates his customary attitude in relation to spiritualistic research. The experiments here mentioned, however, were not satisfactory.

To Mrs. Charles McQuiston:

DOBBS FERRY, N. Y.

March 26, 1901.

DEAR MRS. McQUISTON,—I have never had an experience which moved me to believe the living can communicate with the dead, but my wife and I have experimented in the matter when opportunity offered and shall continue to do so.

I enclose a letter which came this morning—the second from the same source. Mrs. K——is a Missourian, and lately she discovered, by accident, that she was a remarkable hypnotiser. Her best subject is a Missouri girl, Miss White, who is to come here soon and sustain strictly scientific tests before professors at Columbia University. Mrs. Clemens and I intend to be present. And we shall ask the pair to come to our house to do whatever things they can do. Meantime, if you thought well of it, you might write her and arrange a meeting, telling her it is by my suggestion and that I gave you her address.

Someone has told me that Mrs. Piper is discredited. I cannot be sure, but I think it was Mr. Myers, President of the London Psychical Research Society—we heard of his death yesterday. He was a spiritualist. I am afraid he was a very easily convinced man. We visited two mediums whom he and Andrew Lang considered quite wonderful, but they were quite transparent frauds.

Mrs. Clemens corrects me: One of those women was a fraud, the other not a fraud, but only an innocent, well-meaning, driveling vacancy.

Sincerely yours,

S. L. CLEMENS.

In Mark Twain's Bermuda chapters entitled Idle Notes of an Idle Excursion he tells of an old sea captain, one Hurricane Jones, who explained biblical miracles in a practical, even if somewhat startling, fashion. In his story of the prophets of Baal, for instance, the old captain declared that the burning water was nothing more nor less than petroleum. Upon reading the "notes," Professor Phelps of Yale wrote that the same method of explaining miracles had been offered by Sir Thomas Browne.

Perhaps it may be added that Captain Hurricane Jones also appears in Roughing It, as Captain Ned Blakely.

To Professor William Lyon Phelps;

YALE UNIVERSITY,

NEW YORK, April 24, 1901.

MY DEAR SIR,—I was not aware that old Sir Thomas had anticipated that story, and I am much obliged to you for furnishing me the paragraph.

It is curious that the same idea should leave entered two heads so unlike as the head of that wise old philosopher and that of Captain Ned Wakeman, a splendidly uncultured old sailor, but in his own opinion a thinker by divine right. He was an old friend of mine of many years' standing; I made two or three voyages with him, and found him a darling in many ways. The petroleum story was not told to me; he told it to Joe Twichell, who ran across him by accident on a sea voyage where I think the two were the only passengers. A delicious pair, and admirably mated, they took to each other at once and became as thick as thieves. Joe was passing under a fictitious name, and old Wakeman didn't suspect that he was a parson; so he gave his profanity full swing, and he was a master of that great art. You probably know Twichell, and will know that that is a kind of refreshment which he is very capable of enjoying.

Sincerely yours,

S. L. CLEMENS.

For the summer Clemens and his family found a comfortable lodge in the Adirondacks—a log cabin called "The Lair"—on Saranac Lake. Soon after his arrival there he received an invitation to attend the celebration of Missouri's eightieth anniversary. He sent the following letter:

To Edward L. Dimmitt, in St. Louis:

AMONG THE ADIRONDACK LAKES, July 19, 1901.

DEAR MR. DIMMITT,—By an error in the plans, things go wrong end first in this world, and much precious time is lost and matters of urgent importance are fatally retarded. Invitations which a brisk young fellow should get, and which would transport him with joy, are delayed and impeded and obstructed until they are fifty years overdue when they reach him.

It has happened again in this case.

When I was a boy in Missouri I was always on the lookout for invitations but they always miscarried and went wandering through the aisles of time; and now they are arriving when I am old and rheumatic and can't travel and must lose my chance.

I have lost a world of delight through this matter of delaying invitations. Fifty years ago I would have gone eagerly across the world to help celebrate anything that might turn up. IT would have made no difference to me what it was, so that I was there and allowed a chance to make a noise.

The whole scheme of things is turned wrong end to. Life should begin with age and its privileges and accumulations, and end with youth and its capacity to splendidly enjoy such advantages. As things are now, when in youth a dollar would bring a hundred pleasures, you can't have it. When you are old, you get it and there is nothing worth buying with it then.

It's an epitome of life. The first half of it consists of the capacity to enjoy without the chance; the last half consists of the chance without the capacity.

I am admonished in many ways that time is pushing me inexorably along. I am approaching the threshold of age; in 1977 I shall be 142. This is no time to be flitting about the earth. I must cease from the activities proper to youth and begin to take on the dignities and gravities and inertia proper to that season of honorable senility which is on its way and imminent as indicated above.

Yours is a great and memorable occasion, and as a son of Missouri I should hold it a high privilege to be there and share your just pride in the state's achievements; but I must deny myself the indulgence, while thanking you earnestly for the prized honor you have done me in asking me to be present.

Very truly yours,

S. L. CLEMENS.

In the foregoing Mark Twain touches upon one of his favorite fancies: that life should begin with old age and approach strong manhood, golden youth, to end at last with pampered and beloved babyhood. Possibly he contemplated writing a story with this idea as the theme, but He seems never to have done so.

The reader who has followed these letters may remember Yung Wing, who had charge of the Chinese educational mission in Hartford, and how Mark Twain, with Twichell, called on General Grant in behalf of the mission. Yung Wing, now returned to China, had conceived the idea of making an appeal to the Government of the United States for relief of his starving countrymen.

To J. H. Twichell, in Hartford:

AMPERSAND, N. Y., July 28, '01.

DEAR JOE,—As you say, it is impracticable—in my case, certainly. For me to assist in an appeal to that Congress of land-thieves and liars would be to bring derision upon it; and for me to assist in an appeal for cash to pass through the hands of those missionaries out there, of any denomination, Catholic or Protestant, wouldn't do at all. They wouldn't handle money which I had soiled, and I wouldn't trust them with it, anyway. They would devote it to the relief of suffering—I know that—but the sufferers selected would be converts. The missionary-utterances exhibit no humane feeling toward the others, but in place of it a spirit of hate and hostility. And it is natural; the Bible forbids their presence there, their trade is unlawful, why shouldn't their characters be of necessity in harmony with—but never mind, let it go, it irritates me.

Later.... I have been reading Yung Wing's letter again. It may be that he is over-wrought by his sympathies, but it may not be so. There may be other reasons why the missionaries are silent about the Shensi-2-year famine and cannibalism. It may be that there are so few Protestant converts there that the missionaries are able to take care of them. That they are not likely to largely concern themselves about Catholic converts and the others, is quite natural, I think.

That crude way of appealing to this Government for help in a cause which has no money in it, and no politics, rises before me again in all its admirable innocence! Doesn't Yung Wing know us yet? However, he has been absent since '96 or '97. We have gone to hell since then. Kossuth couldn't raise 30 cents in Congress, now, if he were back with his moving Magyar-Tale.

I am on the front porch (lower one—main deck) of our little bijou of a dwelling-house. The lake-edge (Lower Saranac) is so nearly under me that I can't see the shore, but only the water, small-pored with rain-splashes—for there is a heavy down-pour. It is charmingly like sitting snuggled up on a ship's deck with the stretching sea all around—but very much more satisfactory, for at sea a rain-storm is depressing, while here of course the effect engendered is just a deep sense of comfort and contentment. The heavy forest shuts us solidly in on three sides there are no neighbors. There are beautiful little tan-colored impudent squirrels about. They take tea, 5 p. m., (not invited) at the table in the woods where Jean does my typewriting, and one of them has been brave enough to sit upon Jean's knee with his tail curved over his back and munch his food. They come to dinner, 7 p. m., on the front porch (not invited). They all have the one name—Blennerhasset, from Burr's friend—and none of them answers to it except when hungry.

We have been here since June 21st. For a little while we had some warm days—according to the family's estimate; I was hardly discommoded myself. Otherwise the weather has been of the sort you are familiar with in these regions: cool days and cool nights. We have heard of the hot wave every Wednesday, per the weekly paper—we allow no dailies to intrude. Last week through visitors also—the only ones we have had—Dr. Root and John Howells.

We have the daily lake-swim; and all the tribe, servants included (but not I) do a good deal of boating; sometimes with the guide, sometimes without him—Jean and Clara are competent with the oars. If we live another year, I hope we shall spend its summer in this house.

We have taken the Appleton country seat, overlooking the Hudson, at Riverdale, 25 minutes from the Grand Central Station, for a year, beginning Oct. 1, with option for another year. We are obliged to be close to New York for a year or two.

Aug. 3rd. I go yachting a fortnight up north in a 20-knot boat 225 feet long, with the owner, (Mr. Rogers), Tom Reid, Dr. Rice, Col. A. G. Paine and one or two others. Judge Howland would go, but can't get away from engagements; Professor Sloane would go, but is in the grip of an illness. Come—will you go? If you can manage it, drop a post-card to me c/o H.H. Rogers, 26 Broadway. I shall be in New York a couple of days before we sail—July 31 or Aug. 1, perhaps the latter,—and I think I shall stop at the Hotel Grosvenor, cor. 10th St and 5th ave.

We all send you and the Harmonies lots and gobs of love.

MARK

To Rev. J. H. Twichell, in Hartford:

AMPERSAND, N. Y., Aug. 28.

DEAR JOE,—Just a word, to scoff at you, with your extravagant suggestion that I read the biography of Phillips Brooks—the very dullest book that has been printed for a century. Joe, ten pages of Mrs. Cheney's masterly biography of her fathers—no, five pages of it—contain more meat, more sense, more literature, more brilliancy, than that whole basketful of drowsy rubbish put together. Why, in that dead atmosphere even Brooks himself is dull—he wearied me; oh how he wearied me!

We had a noble good time in the Yacht, and caught a Chinese missionary and drowned him.

Love from us all to you all.

MARK.

The assassination of President McKinley occurred September 6, 1901.

Such an event would naturally stir Mark Twain to comment on human nature in general. His letter to Twichell is as individual as it is sound in philosophy. At what period of his own life, or under what circumstances, he made the long journey with tragic intent there is no means of knowing now. There is no other mention of it elsewhere in the records that survive him.

To Rev. J. H. Twichell, in Hartford:

AMPERSAND, Tuesday, (Sept. 10, 1901)

DEAR JOE,—It is another off day, but tomorrow I shall resume work to a certainty, and bid a long farewell to letter-scribbling.

The news of the President looks decidedly hopeful, and we are all glad, and the household faces are much improved, as to cheerfulness. Oh, the talk in the newspapers! Evidently the Human Race is the same old Human Race. And how unjust, and unreflectingly discriminating, the talkers are. Under the unsettling effects of powerful emotion the talkers are saying wild things, crazy things—they are out of themselves, and do not know it; they are temporarily insane, yet with one voice they declare the assassin sane—a man who has been entertaining fiery and reason—debauching maggots in his head for weeks and months. Why, no one is sane, straight along, year in and year out, and we all know it. Our insanities are of varying sorts, and express themselves in varying forms—fortunately harmless forms as a rule—but in whatever form they occur an immense upheaval of feeling can at any time topple us distinctly over the sanity-line for a little while; and then if our form happens to be of the murderous kind we must look out—and so must the spectator.

This ass with the unpronounceable name was probably more insane than usual this week or two back, and may get back upon his bearings by and by, but he was over the sanity-border when he shot the President. It is possible that it has taken him the whole interval since the murder of the King of Italy to get insane enough to attempt the President's life. Without a doubt some thousands of men have been meditating the same act in the same interval, but new and strong interests have intervened and diverted their over-excited minds long enough to give them a chance to settle, and tranquilize, and get back upon a healthy level again. Every extraordinary occurrence unsettles the heads of hundreds of thousands of men for a few moments or hours or days. If there had been ten kings around when Humbert fell they would have been in great peril for a day or more—and from men in whose presence they would have been quite safe after the excess of their excitement had had an interval in which to cool down. I bought a revolver once and travelled twelve hundred miles to kill a man. He was away. He was gone a day. With nothing else to do, I had to stop and think—and did. Within an hour—within half of it—I was ashamed of myself—and felt unspeakably ridiculous. I do not know what to call it if I was not insane. During a whole week my head was in a turmoil night and day fierce enough and exhausting enough to upset a stronger reason than mine.

All over the world, every day, there are some millions of men in that condition temporarily. And in that time there is always a moment—perhaps only a single one when they would do murder if their man was at hand. If the opportunity comes a shade too late, the chances are that it has come permanently too late. Opportunity seldom comes exactly at the supreme moment. This saves a million lives a day in the world—for sure.

No Ruler is ever slain but the tremendous details of it are ravenously devoured by a hundred thousand men whose minds dwell, unaware, near the temporary-insanity frontier—and over they go, now! There is a day—two days—three—during which no Ruler would be safe from perhaps the half of them; and there is a single moment wherein he would not be safe from any of them, no doubt.

It may take this present shooting-case six months to breed another ruler-tragedy, but it will breed it. There is at least one mind somewhere which will brood, and wear, and decay itself to the killing-point and produce that tragedy.

Every negro burned at the stake unsettles the excitable brain of another one—I mean the inflaming details of his crime, and the lurid theatricality of his exit do it—and the duplicate crime follows; and that begets a repetition, and that one another one and so on. Every lynching-account unsettles the brains of another set of excitable white men, and lights another pyre—115 lynchings last year, 102 inside of 8 months this year; in ten years this will be habit, on these terms.

Yes, the wild talk you see in the papers! And from men who are sane when not upset by overwhelming excitement. A U. S. Senator-Cullom—wants this Buffalo criminal lynched! It would breed other lynchings—of men who are not dreaming of committing murders, now, and will commit none if Cullom will keep quiet and not provide the exciting cause.

And a District Attorney wants a law which shall punish with death attempts upon a President's life—this, mind you, as a deterrent. It would have no effect—or the opposite one. The lunatic's mind-space is all occupied—as mine was—with the matter in hand; there is no room in it for reflections upon what may happen to him. That comes after the crime.

It is the noise the attempt would make in the world that would breed the subsequent attempts, by unsettling the rickety minds of men who envy the criminal his vast notoriety—his obscure name tongued by stupendous Kings and Emperors—his picture printed everywhere, the trivialest details of his movements, what he eats, what he drinks; how he sleeps, what he says, cabled abroad over the whole globe at cost of fifty thousand dollars a day—and he only a lowly shoemaker yesterday!—like the assassin of the President of France—in debt three francs to his landlady, and insulted by her—and to-day she is proud to be able to say she knew him "as familiarly as you know your own brother," and glad to stand till she drops and pour out columns and pages of her grandeur and her happiness upon the eager interviewer.

Nothing will check the lynchings and ruler-murder but absolute silence—the absence of pow-pow about them. How are you going to manage that? By gagging every witness and jamming him into a dungeon for life; by abolishing all newspapers; by exterminating all newspaper men; and by extinguishing God's most elegant invention, the Human Race. It is quite simple, quite easy, and I hope you will take a day off and attend to it, Joe. I blow a kiss to you, and am

Lovingly Yours,

MARK.

When the Adirondack summer ended Clemens settled for the winter in the beautiful Appleton home at Riverdale-on-the-Hudson. It was a place of wide-spreading grass and shade-a house of ample room. They were established in it in time for Mark Twain to take an active interest in the New York elections and assist a ticket for good government to defeat Tammany Hall.

XLI. LETTERS OF 1902. RIVERDALE. YORK HARBOR. ILLNESS OF MRS. CLEMENS

The year 1902 was an eventful one for Mark Twain. In April he received a degree of LL.D. from the University of Missouri and returned to his native State to accept it. This was his last journey to the Mississippi River. During the summer Mrs. Clemens's health broke down and illnesses of one sort or another visited other members of the family. Amid so much stress and anxiety Clemens had little time or inclination for work. He wrote not many letters and mainly somber ones. Once, by way of diversion, he worked out the idea of a curious club—which he formed—its members to be young girls—girls for the most part whom he had never seen. They were elected without their consent from among those who wrote to him without his consent, and it is not likely that any one so chosen declined membership. One selection from his letters to the French member, Miss Helene Picard, of St.-Die, France, will explain the club and present a side of Mask Twain somewhat different from that found in most of his correspondence.

To Miss Picard, in St.-Die, France:

RIVERDALE-ON-THE-HUDSON, February 22, 1902.

DEAR MISS HELENE,—If you will let me call you so, considering that my head is white and that I have grownup daughters. Your beautiful letter has given me such deep pleasure! I will make bold to claim you for a friend and lock you up with the rest of my riches; for I am a miser who counts his spoil every day and hoards it secretly and adds to it when he can, and is grateful to see it grow.

Some of that gold comes, like yourself, in a sealed package, and I can't see it and may never have the happiness; but I know its value without that, and by what sum it increases my wealth.

I have a Club, a private Club, which is all my own. I appoint the

Members myself, and they can't help themselves, because I don't allow them to vote on their own appointment and I don't allow them to resign! They are all friends whom I have never seen (save one), but who have written friendly letters to me.

By the laws of my Club there can be only one Member in each country, and there can be no male Member but myself. Some day I may admit males, but I don't know—they are capricious and inharmonious, and their ways provoke me a good deal. It is a matter which the Club shall decide.

I have made four appointments in the past three or four months: You as Member for France, a young Highland girl as Member for Scotland, a Mohammedan girl as Member for Bengal, and a dear and bright young niece of mine as Member for the United States—for I do not represent a country myself, but am merely Member at Large for the Human Race.

You must not try to resign, for the laws of the Club do not allow that. You must console yourself by remembering that you are in the best of company; that nobody knows of your membership except myself—that no Member knows another's name, but only her country; that no taxes are levied and no meetings held (but how dearly I should like to attend one!).

One of my Members is a Princess of a royal house, another is the daughter of a village book-seller on the continent of Europe. For the only qualification for Membership is intellect and the spirit of good will; other distinctions, hereditary or acquired, do not count.

May I send you the Constitution and Laws of the Club? I shall be so pleased if I may. It is a document which one of my daughters typewrites for me when I need one for a new Member, and she would give her eyebrows to know what it is all about, but I strangle her curiosity by saying: "There are much cheaper typewriters than you are, my dear, and if you try to pry into the sacred mysteries of this Club one of your prosperities will perish sure."

My favorite? It is "Joan of Arc." My next is "Huckleberry Finn," but the family's next is "The Prince and the Pauper." (Yes, you are right—I am a moralist in disguise; it gets me into heaps of trouble when I go thrashing around in political questions.)

I wish you every good fortune and happiness and I thank you so much for your letter.

Sincerely yours,

S. L. CLEMENS.

Early in the year Clemens paid a visit to Twichell in Hartford, and after one of their regular arguments on theology and the moral accountability of the human race, arguments that had been going on between them for more than thirty years—Twichell lent his visitor Freedom of the Will, by Jonathan Edwards, to read on the way home. The next letter was the result.

To Rev. J. H. Twichell, in Hartford:

RIVERDALE-ON-THE-HUDSON.

Feb. '02.

DEAR JOE,—"After compliments."—[Meaning "What a good time you gave me; what a happiness it was to be under your roof again; etc., etc." See opening sentence of all translations of letters passing between Lord Roberts and Indian princes and rulers.]—From Bridgeport to New York; thence to home; and continuously until near midnight I wallowed and reeked with Jonathan in his insane debauch; rose immediately refreshed and fine at 10 this morning, but with a strange and haunting sense of having been on a three days' tear with a drunken lunatic. It is years since I have known these sensations. All through the book is the glaze of a resplendent intellect gone mad—a marvelous spectacle. No, not all through the book—the drunk does not come on till the last third, where what I take to be Calvinism and its God begins to show up and shine red and hideous in the glow from the fires of hell, their only right and proper adornment. By God I was ashamed to be in such company.

Jonathan seems to hold (as against the Arminian position) that the Man (or his Soul or his Will) never creates an impulse itself, but is moved to action by an impulse back of it. That's sound!

Also, that of two or more things offered it, it infallibly chooses the one which for the moment is most pleasing to ITSELF. Perfectly correct! An immense admission for a man not otherwise sane.

Up to that point he could have written chapters III and IV of my suppressed "Gospel." But there we seem to separate. He seems to concede the indisputable and unshakable dominion of Motive and Necessity (call them what he may, these are exterior forces and not under the man's authority, guidance or even suggestion)—then he suddenly flies the logic track and (to all seeming) makes the man and not these exterior forces responsible to God for the man's thoughts, words and acts. It is frank insanity.

I think that when he concedes the autocratic dominion of Motive and Necessity he grants, a third position of mine—that a man's mind is a mere machine—an automatic machine—which is handled entirely from the outside, the man himself furnishing it absolutely nothing: not an ounce of its fuel, and not so much as a bare suggestion to that exterior engineer as to what the machine shall do, nor how it shall do it nor when.

After that concession, it was time for him to get alarmed and shirk—for he was pointing straight for the only rational and possible next-station on that piece of road the irresponsibility of man to God.

And so he shirked. Shirked, and arrived at this handsome result:

Man is commanded to do so-and-so. It has been ordained from the beginning of time that some men shan't and others can't.

These are to be blamed: let them be damned.

I enjoy the Colonel very much, and shall enjoy the rest of him with an obscene delight.

Joe, the whole tribe shout love to you and yours!

MARK.

We have not heard of Joe Goodman since the trying days of '90 and '91, when he was seeking to promote the fortunes of the type-setting machine. Goodman, meantime, who had in turn been miner, printer, publisher, and farmer; had been devoting his energies and genius to something entirely new: he had been translating the prehistoric Mayan inscriptions of Yucatan, and with such success that his work was elaborately published by an association of British scientists. In due time a copy of this publication came to Clemens, who was full of admiration of the great achievement.

To J. T. Goodman, in California:

RIVERDALE-ON-THE-HUDSON,

June 13, '02.

DEAR JOE,—I am lost in reverence and admiration! It is now twenty-four hours that I have been trying to cool down and contemplate with quiet blood this extraordinary spectacle of energy, industry, perseverance, pluck, analytical genius, penetration, this irruption of thunders and fiery splendors from a fair and flowery mountain that nobody had supposed was a sleeping volcano, but I seem to be as excited as ever. Yesterday I read as much as half of the book, not understanding a word but enchanted nevertheless—partly by the wonder of it all, the study, the erudition, the incredible labor, the modesty, the dignity, the majestic exclusiveness of the field and its lofty remoteness from things and contacts sordid and mean and earthy, and partly by the grace and beauty and limpidity of the book's unsurpassable English. Science, always great and worshipful, goes often in hodden grey, but you have clothed her in garments meet for her high degree.

You think you get "poor pay" for your twenty years? No, oh no. You have lived in a paradise of the intellect whose lightest joys were beyond the reach of the longest purse in Christendom, you have had daily and nightly emancipation from the world's slaveries and gross interests, you have received a bigger wage than any man in the land, you have dreamed a splendid dream and had it come true, and to-day you could not afford to trade fortunes with anybody—not even with another scientist, for he must divide his spoil with his guild, whereas essentially the world you have discovered is your own and must remain so.

It is all just magnificent, Joe! And no one is prouder or gladder than

Yours always

MARK.

At York Harbor, Maine, where they had taken a cottage for the summer—a pretty place, with Howells not far distant, at Kittery Point—Mrs. Clemens's health gave way. This was at a period when telegraphic communication was far from reliable. The old-time Western Union had fallen from grace; its "system" no longer justified the best significance of that word. The new day of reorganization was coming, and it was time for it. Mark Twain's letter concerning the service at York Harbor would hardly be warranted today, but those who remember conditions of that earlier time will agree that it was justified then, and will appreciate its satire.

To the President of The Western Union, in New York:

"THE PINES"

YORK HARBOR, MAINE.

DEAR SIR,—I desire to make a complaint, and I bring it to you, the head of the company, because by experience I know better than to carry it to a subordinate.

I have been here a month and a half, and by testimony of friends, reinforced by personal experience I now feel qualified to claim as an established fact that the telegraphic service here is the worst in the world except that Boston.

These services are actually slower than was the New York and Hartford service in the days when I last complained to you—which was fifteen or eighteen years ago, when telegraphic time and train time between the mentioned points was exactly the same, to-wit, three hours and a half. Six days ago—it was that raw day which provoked so much comment—my daughter was on her way up from New York, and at noon she telegraphed me from New Haven asking that I meet her with a cloak at Portsmouth. Her telegram reached me four hours and a quarter later—just 15 minutes too late for me to catch my train and meet her.

I judge that the telegram traveled about 200 miles. It is the best telegraphic work I have seen since I have been here, and I am mentioning it in this place not as a complaint but as a compliment. I think a compliment ought always to precede a complaint, where one is possible, because it softens resentment and insures for the complaint a courteous and gentle reception.

Still, there is a detail or two connected with this matter which ought perhaps to be mentioned. And now, having smoothed the way with the compliment, I will venture them. The head corpse in the York Harbor office sent me that telegram altho (1) he knew it would reach me too late to be of any value; (2) also, that he was going to send it to me by his boy; (3) that the boy would not take the trolley and come the 2 miles in 12 minutes, but would walk; (4) that he would be two hours and a quarter on the road; (5) and that he would collect 25 cents for transportation, for a telegram which the he knew to be worthless before he started it. From these data I infer that the Western Union owes me 75 cents; that is to say, the amount paid for combined wire and land transportation—a recoup provided for in the printed paragraph which heads the telegraph-blank.

By these humane and Christian stages we now arrive at the complaint proper. We have had a grave case of illness in the family, and a relative was coming some six hundred miles to help in the sick-room during the convalescing period. It was an anxious time, of course, and I wrote and asked to be notified as to the hour of the expected arrival of this relative in Boston or in York Harbor. Being afraid of the telegraph—which I think ought not to be used in times of hurry and emergency—I asked that the desired message be brought to me by some swift method of transportation. By the milkman, if he was coming this way. But there are always people who think they know more than you do, especially young people; so of course the young fellow in charge of this lady used the telegraph. And at Boston, of all places! Except York Harbor.

The result was as usual; let me employ a statelier and exacter term, and say, historical.

The dispatch was handed to the h. c. of the Boston office at 9 this morning. It said, "Shall bring A. S. to you eleven forty-five this morning." The distance traveled by the dispatch is forty or fifty miles, I suppose, as the train-time is five minutes short of two hours, and the trains are so slow that they can't give a W. U. telegram two hours and twenty minutes start and overtake it.

As I have said, the dispatch was handed in at Boston at 9. The expected visitors left Boston at 9.40, and reached my house at 12 noon, beating the telegram 2 solid hours, and 5 minutes over.

The boy brought the telegram. It was bald-headed with age, but still legible. The boy was prostrate with travel and exposure, but still alive, and I went out to condole with him and get his last wishes and send for the ambulance. He was waiting to collect transportation before turning his passing spirit to less serious affairs. I found him strangely intelligent, considering his condition and where he is getting his training. I asked him at what hour the telegram was handed to the h. c. in Boston. He answered brightly, that he didn't know.

I examined the blank, and sure enough the wary Boston h. c. had thoughtfully concealed that statistic. I asked him at what hour it had started from Boston. He answered up as brightly as ever, and said he didn't know.

I examined the blank, and sure enough the Boston h. c. had left that statistic out in the cold, too. In fact it turned out to be an official concealment—no blank was provided for its exposure. And none required by the law, I suppose. "It is a good one-sided idea," I remarked; "They can take your money and ship your telegram next year if they want to—you've no redress. The law ought to extend the privilege to all of us."

The boy looked upon me coldly.

I asked him when the telegram reached York Harbor. He pointed to some figures following the signature at the bottom of the blank—"12.14." I said it was now 1.45 and asked—

"Do you mean that it reached your morgue an hour and a half ago?"

He nodded assent.

"It was at that time half an hour too late to be of any use to me, if I wanted to go and meet my people—which was the case—for by the wording of the message you can see that they were to arrive at the station at 11.45. Why did, your h. c. send me this useless message? Can't he read? Is he dead?"

"It's the rules."

"No, that does not account for it. Would he have sent it if it had been three years old, I in the meantime deceased, and he aware of it?"

The boy didn't know.

"Because, you know, a rule which required him to forward to the cemetery to-day a dispatch due three years ago, would be as good a rule as one which should require him to forward a telegram to me to-day which he knew had lost all its value an hour or two before he started it. The construction of such a rule would discredit an idiot; in fact an idiot—I mean a common ordinary Christian idiot, you understand—would be ashamed of it, and for the sake of his reputation wouldn't make it. What do you think?"

He replied with much natural brilliancy that he wasn't paid for thinking.

This gave me a better opinion of the commercial intelligence pervading his morgue than I had had before; it also softened my feelings toward him, and also my tone, which had hitherto been tinged with bitterness.

"Let bygones be bygones," I said, gently, "we are all erring creatures, and mainly idiots, but God made us so and it is dangerous to criticise."

Sincerely

S. L. CLEMENS.

One day there arrived from Europe a caller with a letter of introduction from Elizabeth, Queen of Rumania, better known as Carmen Sylva. The visitor was Madam Hartwig, formerly an American girl, returning now, because of reduced fortunes, to find profitable employment in her own land. Her husband, a man of high principle, had declined to take part in an "affair of honor," as recognized by the Continental code; hence his ruin. Elizabeth of Rumania was one of the most loved and respected of European queens and an author of distinction. Mark Twain had known her in Vienna. Her letter to him and his own letter to the public (perhaps a second one, for its date is two years later) follow herewith.

From Carmen Sylva to Mark Twain:

BUCAREST, May 9, 1902.

HONORED MASTER,—If I venture to address you on behalf of a poor lady, who is stranded in Bucarest I hope not to be too disagreeable.

Mrs. Hartwig left America at the age of fourteen in order to learn to sing which she has done thoroughly. Her husband had quite a brilliant situation here till he refused to partake 'dans une afaire onereuse', so it seems. They haven't a penny and each of them must try to find a living. She is very nice and pleasant and her school is so good that she most certainly can give excellent singing lessons.

I beg your pardon for being a bore to one I so deeply love and admire, to whom I owe days and days of forgetfulness of self and troubles and the intensest of all joys: Hero-worship! People don't always realize what a happiness that is! God bless you for every beautiful thought you poured into my tired heart and for every smile on a weary way!

CARMEN SYLVA.

From Mark Twain to the Public:

Nov. 16, '04.

TO WHOM IT MAY CONCERN,—I desire to recommend Madame Hartwig to my friends and the public as a teacher of singing and as a concert-vocalist. She has lived for fifteen years at the court of Roumania, and she brought with her to America an autograph letter in which her Majesty the Queen of Roumania cordially certified her to me as being an accomplished and gifted singer and teacher of singing, and expressed a warm hope that her professional venture among us would meet with success; through absence in Europe I have had no opportunity to test the validity of the Queen's judgment in the matter, but that judgment is the utterance of an entirely competent authority—the best that occupies a throne, and as good as any that sits elsewhere, as the musical world well knows—and therefore back it without hesitation, and endorse it with confidence.

I will explain that the reason her Majesty tried to do her friend a friendly office through me instead of through someone else was, not that I was particularly the right or best person for the office, but because I was not a stranger. It is true that I am a stranger to some of the monarchs—mainly through their neglect of their opportunities—but such is not the case in the present instance. The latter fact is a high compliment to me, and perhaps I ought to conceal it. Some people would.

MARK TWAIN.

Mrs. Clemens's improvement was scarcely perceptible. It was not until October that they were able to remove her to Riverdale, and then only in a specially arranged invalid-car. At the end of the long journey she was carried to her room and did not leave it again for many months.

To Rev. J. H. Twichell, in Hartford:

RIVERDALE, N. Y., Oct. 31, '02.

DEAR JOE,—It is ten days since Susy [Twichell] wrote that you were laid up with a sprained shoulder, since which time we have had no news about it. I hope that no news is good news, according to the proverb; still, authoritative confirmation of it will be gladly received in this family, if some of you will furnish it. Moreover, I should like to know how and where it happened. In the pulpit, as like as not, otherwise you would not be taking so much pains to conceal it. This is not a malicious suggestion, and not a personally-invented one: you told me yourself, once, that you threw artificial power and impressiveness into places in your sermons where needed, by "banging the bible"—(your own words.) You have reached a time of life when it is not wise to take these risks. You would better jump around. We all have to change our methods as the infirmities of age creep upon us. Jumping around will be impressive now, whereas before you were gray it would have excited remark.

Poor Livy drags along drearily. It must be hard times for that turbulent spirit. It will be a long time before she is on her feet again. It is a most pathetic case. I wish I could transfer it to myself. Between ripping and raging and smoking and reading, I could get a good deal of a holiday out of it.

Clara runs the house smoothly and capably. She is discharging a trial-cook today and hiring another.

A power of love to you all!

MARK.

Such was the state of Mrs. Clemens's health that visitors were excluded from the sick room, and even Clemens himself was allowed to see her no more than a few moments at a time. These brief, precious visits were the chief interests of his long days. Occasionally he was allowed to send her a few lines, reporting his occupations, and these she was sometimes permitted to answer. Only one of his notes has been preserved, written after a day, now rare, of literary effort. Its signature, the letter Y, stands for "Youth," always her name for him.

To Mrs. Clemens:

DEAR HEART,—I've done another full day's work, and finished before 4. I have been reading and dozing since and would have had a real sleep a few minutes ago but for an incursion to bring me a couple of unimportant letters. I've stuck to the bed all day and am getting back my lost ground. Next time I will be strictly careful and make my visit very short—just a kiss and a rush. Thank you for your dear, dear note; you who are my own and only sweetheart.

Sleep well!

Y.

XLII. LETTERS OF 1903. TO VARIOUS PERSONS. HARD DAYS AT RIVERDALE. LAST SUMMER AT ELMIRA. THE RETURN TO ITALY.

The reader may perhaps recall that H. H. Rogers, some five or six years earlier, had taken charge of the fortunes of Helen Keller, making it possible for her to complete her education. Helen had now written her first book—a wonderful book—'The Story of My Life', and it had been successfully published. For a later generation it may be proper to explain that the Miss Sullivan, later Mrs. Macy, mentioned in the letter which follows, was the noble woman who had devoted her life to the enlightenment of this blind, dumb girl—had made it possible for her to speak and understand, and, indeed, to see with the eyes of luminous imagination.

The case of plagiarism mentioned in this letter is not now remembered, and does not matter, but it furnished a text for Mark Twain, whose remarks on the subject in general are eminently worth while.

To Helen Keller, in Wrentham, Mass.:

RIVERDALE-ON-THE-HUDSON,

ST. PATRICK'S DAY, '03.

DEAR HELEN,—I must steal half a moment from my work to say how glad I am to have your book, and how highly I value it, both for its own sake and as a remembrances of an affectionate friendship which has subsisted between us for nine years without a break, and without a single act of violence that I can call to mind. I suppose there is nothing like it in heaven; and not likely to be, until we get there and show off. I often think of it with longing, and how they'll say, "There they come—sit down in front!" I am practicing with a tin halo. You do the same. I was at Henry Rogers's last night, and of course we talked of you. He is not at all well; you will not like to hear that; but like you and me, he is just as lovely as ever.

I am charmed with your book-enchanted. You are a wonderful creature, the most wonderful in the world—you and your other half together—Miss Sullivan, I mean, for it took the pair of you to make a complete and perfect whole. How she stands out in her letters! her brilliancy, penetration, originality, wisdom, character, and the fine literary competencies of her pen—they are all there.

Oh, dear me, how unspeakably funny and owlishly idiotic and grotesque was that "plagiarism" farce! As if there was much of anything in any human utterance, oral or written, except plagiarism! The kernel, the soul—let us go further and say the substance, the bulk, the actual and valuable material of all human utterances—is plagiarism. For substantially all ideas are second-hand, consciously and unconsciously drawn from a million outside sources, and daily used by the garnerer with a pride and satisfaction born of the superstition that he originated them; whereas there is not a rag of originality about them anywhere except the little discoloration they get from his mental and moral calibre and his temperament, and which is revealed in characteristics of phrasing. When a great orator makes a great speech you are listening to ten centuries and ten thousand men—but we call it his speech, and really some exceedingly small portion of it is his. But not enough to signify. It is merely a Waterloo. It is Wellington's battle, in some degree, and we call it his; but there are others that contributed. It takes a thousand men to invent a telegraph, or a steam engine, or a phonograph, or a photograph, or a telephone or any other important thing—and the last man gets the credit and we forget the others. He added his little mite—that is all he did. These object lessons should teach us that ninety-nine parts of all things that proceed from the intellect are plagiarisms, pure and simple; and the lesson ought to make us modest. But nothing can do that.

Then why don't we unwittingly reproduce the phrasing of a story, as well as the story itself? It can hardly happen—to the extent of fifty words except in the case of a child: its memory-tablet is not lumbered with impressions, and the actual language can have graving-room there, and preserve the language a year or two, but a grown person's memory-tablet is a palimpsest, with hardly a bare space upon which to engrave a phrase. It must be a very rare thing that a whole page gets so sharply printed upon a man's mind, by a single reading, that it will stay long enough to turn up some time or other and be mistaken by him for his own. No doubt we are constantly littering our literature with disconnected sentences borrowed from books at some unremembered time and now imagined to be our own, but that is about the most we can do. In 1866 I read Dr. Holmes's poems, in the Sandwich Islands. A year and a half later I stole his dictation, without knowing it, and used it to dedicate my "Innocents Abroad" with. Then years afterwards I was talking with Dr. Holmes about it. He was not an ignorant ass—no, not he: he was not a collection of decayed human turnips, like your "Plagiarism Court;" and so when I said, "I know now where I stole it, but whom did you steal it from," he said, "I don't remember; I only know I stole it from somebody, because I have never originated anything altogether myself, nor met anybody who had."

To think of those solemn donkeys breaking a little child's heart with their ignorant rubbish about plagiarism! I couldn't sleep for blaspheming about it last night. Why, their whole lives, their whole histories, all their learning, all their thoughts, all their opinions were one solid ruck of plagiarism, and they didn't know it and never suspected it. A gang of dull and hoary pirates piously setting themselves the task of disciplining and purifying a kitten that they think they've caught filching a chop! Oh, dam—

But you finish it, dear, I am running short of vocabulary today. Ever lovingly your friend,

MARK.

(Edited and modified by Clara Clemens, deputy to her mother, who for more than 7 months has been ill in bed and unable to exercise her official function.)

The burden of the Clemens household had fallen almost entirely upon Clara Clemens. In addition to supervising its customary affairs, she also shouldered the responsibility of an unusual combination of misfortunes, for besides the critical condition of her mother, her sister, Jean Clemens, was down with pneumonia, no word of which must come to Mrs. Clemens. Certainly it was a difficult position. In some account of it, which he set down later, Clemens wrote: "It was fortunate for us all that Clara's reputation for truthfulness was so well established in her mother's mind. It was our daily protection from disaster. The mother never doubted Clara's word. Clara could tell her large improbabilities without exciting any suspicion, whereas if I tried to market even a small and simple one the case would have been different. I was never able to get a reputation like Clara's."

The accumulation of physical ailments in the Clemens home had somewhat modified Mark Twain's notion of medical practice. He was no longer radical; he had become eclectic. It is a good deal of a concession that he makes to Twichell, after those earlier letters from Sweden, in which osteopathy had been heralded as the anodyne for all human ills.

To Rev. J. H. Twichell, in Hartford:

DEAR JOE,—Livy does really make a little progress these past 3 or 4 days, progress which is visible to even the untrained eye. The physicians are doing good work with her, but my notion is, that no art of healing is the best for all ills. I should distribute the ailments around: surgery cases to the surgeons; lupus to the actinic-ray specialist; nervous prostration to the Christian Scientist; most ills to the allopath and the homeopath; (in my own particular case) rheumatism, gout and bronchial attacks to the osteopathist.

Mr. Rogers was to sail southward this morning—and here is this weather! I am sorry. I think it's a question if he gets away tomorrow.

Ys Ever

MARK.

It was through J. Y. M. MacAlister, to whom the next letter is written, that Mark Twain had become associated with the Plasmon Company, which explains the reference to "shares." He had seen much of MacAlister during the winter at Tedworth Square, and had grown fond of him. It is a characteristic letter, and one of interesting fact.

To J. Y. M. MacAlister, in London:

RIVERDALE, NEW YORK.

April, 7, '03.

DEAR MACALISTER,—Yours arrived last night, and God knows I was glad to get it, for I was afraid I had blundered into an offence in some way and forfeited your friendship—a kind of blunder I have made so many times in my life that I am always standing in a waiting and morbid dread of its occurrence.

Three days ago I was in condition—during one horribly long night—to sympathetically roast with you in your "hell of troubles." During that night I was back again where I was in the black days when I was buried under a mountain of debt. I called the daughters to me in private council and paralysed them with the announcement, "Our outgo has increased in the past 8 months until our expenses are now 125 per cent. greater than our income."

It was a mistake. When I came down in the morning a gray and aged wreck, and went over the figures again, I found that in some unaccountable way (unaccountable to a business man but not to me) I had multiplied the totals by 2. By God I dropped 75 years on the floor where I stood.

Do you know it affected me as one is affected when he wakes out of a hideous dream and finds that it was only a dream. It was a great comfort and satisfaction to me to call the daughters to a private meeting of the Board again and say, "You need not worry any more; our outgo is only a third more than our income; in a few months your mother will be out of her bed and on her feet again—then we shall drop back to normal and be all right."

Certainly there is a blistering and awful reality about a well-arranged unreality. It is quite within the possibilities that two or three nights like that night of mine could drive a man to suicide. He would refuse to examine the figures; they would revolt him so, and he could go to his death unaware that there was nothing serious about them. I cannot get that night out of my head, it was so vivid, so real, so ghastly. In any other year of these 33 the relief would have been simple: go where you can cut your cloth to fit your income. You can't do that when your wife can't be moved, even from one room to the next.

Clam spells the trained nurse afternoons; I am allowed to see Mrs. Clemens 20 minutes twice a day and write her two letters a day provided I put no news in them. No other person ever sees her except the physician and now and then a nerve-specialist from New York. She saw there was something the matter that morning, but she got no facts out of me. But that is nothing—she hasn't had anything but lies for 8 months. A fact would give her a relapse.

The doctor and a specialist met in conspiracy five days ago, and in their belief she will by and by come out of this as good as new, substantially. They ordered her to Italy for next winter—which seems to indicate that by autumn she will be able to undertake the voyage. So Clara is writing a Florence friend to take a look round among the villas for us in the regions near that city. It seems early to do this, but Joan Bergheim thought it would be wise.

He and his wife lunched with us here yesterday. They have been abroad in Havana 4 months, and they sailed for England this morning.

I am enclosing an order for half of my (your) Founders shares. You are not to refuse them this time, though you have done it twice before. They are yours, not mine, and for your family's sake if not your own you cannot in these cloudy days renounce this property which is so clearly yours and theirs. You have been generous long enough; be just, now to yourself. Mr. Rogers is off yachting for 5 or 6 weeks—I'll get them when he returns. The head of the house joins me in warmest greetings and remembrances to you and Mrs. MacAlister.

Ever yours,

Mark.

May 8. Great Scott! I never mailed this letter! I addressed it, put "Registered" on it—then left it lying unsealed on the arm of my chair, and rushed up to my bed quaking with a chill. I've never been out of the bed since—oh, bronchitis, rheumatism, two sets of teeth aching, land, I've had a dandy time for 4 weeks. And to-day—great guns, one of the very worst!...

I'm devilish sorry, and I do apologise—for although I am not as slow as you are about answering letters, as a rule, I see where I'm standing this time.

Two weeks ago Jean was taken down again—this time with measles, and I haven't been able to go to her and she hasn't been able to come to me.

But Mrs. Clemens is making nice progress, and can stand alone a moment or two at a time.

Now I'll post this.

MARK

The two letters that follow, though written only a few days apart, were separated in their arrival by a period of seven years. The second letter was, in some way, mislaid and not mailed; and it was not until after the writer of it was dead that it was found and forwarded.

Mark Twain could never get up much enthusiasm for the writings of Scott. His praise of Quentin Durward is about the only approval he ever accorded to the works of the great romanticist.

To Brander Matthews, in New York:

NEW YORK CITY, May 4, '03.

DEAR BRANDER,—I haven't been out of my bed for four weeks, but—well, I have been reading, a good deal, and it occurs to me to ask you to sit down, some time or other when you have 8 or 9 months to spare, and jot me down a certain few literary particulars for my help and elevation. Your time need not be thrown away, for at your further leisure you can make Colombian lectures out of the results and do your students a good turn.

1. Are there in Sir Walter's novels passages done in good English—English which is neither slovenly or involved?

2. Are there passages whose English is not poor and thin and commonplace, but is of a quality above that?

3. Are there passages which burn with real fire—not punk, fox-fire, make believe?

4. Has he heroes and heroines who are not cads and cadesses?

5. Has he personages whose acts and talk correspond with their characters as described by him?

6. Has he heroes and heroines whom the reader admires, admires, and knows why?

7. Has he funny characters that are funny, and humorous passages that are humorous?

8. Does he ever chain the reader's interest, and make him reluctant to lay the book down?

9. Are there pages where he ceases from posing, ceases from admiring the placid flood and flow of his own dilutions, ceases from being artificial, and is for a time, long or short, recognizably sincere and in earnest?

10. Did he know how to write English, and didn't do it because he didn't want to?

11. Did he use the right word only when he couldn't think of another one, or did he run so much to wrong because he didn't know the right one when he saw it?

13. Can you read him? and keep your respect for him? Of course a person could in his day—an era of sentimentality and sloppy romantics—but land! can a body do it today?

Brander, I lie here dying, slowly dying, under the blight of Sir Walter. I have read the first volume of Rob Roy, and as far as chapter XIX of Guy Mannering, and I can no longer hold my head up nor take my nourishment. Lord, it's all so juvenile! so artificial, so shoddy; and such wax figures and skeletons and spectres. Interest? Why, it is impossible to feel an interest in these bloodless shams, these milk-and-water humbugs. And oh, the poverty of the invention! Not poverty in inventing situations, but poverty in furnishing reasons for them. Sir Walter usually gives himself away when he arranges for a situation—elaborates, and elaborates, and elaborates, till if you live to get to it you don't believe in it when it happens.

I can't find the rest of Rob Roy, I can't stand any more Mannering—I do not know just what to do, but I will reflect, and not quit this great study rashly. He was great, in his day, and to his proper audience; and so was God in

Jewish times, for that matter, but why should either of them rank high now? And do they?—honest, now, do they? Dam'd if I believe it.

My, I wish I could see you and Leigh Hunt!

Sincerely Yours

S. L. CLEMENS.

To Brander Matthews, in New York:

RIVERDALE, May 8, '03 (Mailed June, 1910).

DEAR BRANDER,—I'm still in bed, but the days have lost their dulness since I broke into Sir Walter and lost my temper. I finished Guy Mannering—that curious, curious book, with its mob of squalid shadows jabbering around a single flesh-and-blood being—Dinmont; a book crazily put together out of the very refuse of the romance-artist's stage properties—finished it and took up Quentin Durward, and finished that.

It was like leaving the dead to mingle with the living: it was like withdrawing from the infant class in the College of journalism to sit under the lectures in English literature in Columbia University.

I wonder who wrote Quentin Durward?

Yrs ever

MARK.

In 1903, preparations were going on for a great world's fair, to be held in St. Louis, and among other features proposed was a World's Literary Convention, with a week to be set apart in honor of Mark Twain, and a special Mark Twain Day in it, on which the National Association would hold grand services in honor of the distinguished Missourian. A letter asking his consent to the plan brought the following reply.

To T. F. Gatts, of Missouri:

NEW YORK, May 30, 1903.

DEAR MR. GATTS,—It is indeed a high compliment which you offer me in naming an association after me and in proposing the setting apart of a Mark Twain day at the great St. Louis fair, but such compliments are not proper for the living; they are proper and safe for the dead only. I value the impulse which moves you to tender me these honors. I value it as highly as any one can, and am grateful for it, but I should stand in a sort of terror of the honors themselves. So long as we remain alive we are not safe from doing things which, however righteously and honorably intended, can wreck our repute and extinguish our friendships.

I hope that no society will be named for me while I am still alive, for I might at some time or other do something which would cause its members to regret having done me that honor. After I shall have joined the dead I shall follow the customs of those people and be guilty of no conduct that can wound any friend; but until that time shall come I shall be a doubtful quantity like the rest of our race.

Very truly yours,

S. L. CLEMENS.

The National Mark Twain Association did not surrender easily. Mr. Gatts wrote a second letter full of urgent appeal. If Mark Twain was tempted, we get no hint of it in his answer.

To T. F. Gatts, of Missouri:

NEW YORK, June 8, 1903.

DEAR MR. GATTS,—While I am deeply touched by the desire of my friends of Hannibal to confer these great honors upon me, I must still forbear to accept them. Spontaneous and unpremeditated honors, like those which came to me at Hannibal, Columbia, St. Louis and at the village stations all down the line, are beyond all price and are a treasure for life in the memory, for they are a free gift out of the heart and they come without solicitations; but I am a Missourian and so I shrink from distinctions which have to be arranged beforehand and with my privity, for I then became a party to my own exalting. I am humanly fond of honors that happen but chary of those that come by canvass and intention. With sincere thanks to you and your associates for this high compliment which you have been minded to offer me, I am,

Very truly yours,

S. L. CLEMENS.

We have seen in the letter to MacAlister that Mark Twain's wife had been ordered to Italy and plans were in progress for an establishment there. By the end of June Mrs. Clemens was able to leave Riverdale, and she made the journey to Quarry Farm, Elmira, where they would remain until October, the month planned for their sailing. The house in Hartford had been sold; and a house which, prior to Mrs. Clemens's breakdown they had bought near Tarrytown (expecting to settle permanently on the Hudson) had been let. They were going to Europe for another indefinite period.

At Quarry Farm Mrs. Clemens continued to improve, and Clemens, once more able to work, occupied the study which Mrs. Crane had built for him thirty years before, and where Tom Sawyer and Huck Finn and the Wandering Prince had been called into being.

To Rev. J. H. Twichell, in Hartford, Conn.:

QUARRY FARM, ELMIRA, N. Y.,

July 21, '03.

DEAR JOE,—That love-letter delighted Livy beyond any like utterance received by her these thirty years and more. I was going to answer it for her right away, and said so; but she reserved the privilege to herself. I judge she is accumulating Hot Stuff—as George Ade would say....

Livy is coming along: eats well, sleeps some, is mostly very gay, not very often depressed; spends all day on the porch, sleeps there a part of the night, makes excursions in carriage and in wheel-chair; and, in the matter of superintending everything and everybody, has resumed business at the old stand.

Did you ever go house-hunting 3,000 miles away? It costs three months of writing and telegraphing to pull off a success. We finished 3 or 4 days ago, and took the Villa Papiniano (dam the name, I have to look at it a minutes after writing it, and then am always in doubt) for a year by cable. Three miles outside of Florence, under Fiesole—a darling location, and apparently a choice house, near Fiske.

There's 7 in our gang. All women but me. It means trunks and things. But thanks be! To-day (this is private) comes a most handsome voluntary document with seals and escutcheons on it from the Italian Ambassador (who is a stranger to me) commanding the Customs people to keep their hands off the Clemens's things. Now wasn't it lovely of him? And wasn't it lovely of me to let Livy take a pencil and edit my answer and knock a good third of it out?

And that's a nice ship—the Irene! new—swift—13,000 tons—rooms up in the sky, open to sun and air—and all that. I was desperately troubled for Livy—about the down-cellar cells in the ancient "Latin."

The cubs are in Riverdale, yet; they come to us the first week in August.

With lots and lots of love to you all,

MARK.

The arrangement for the Villa Papiniano was not completed, after all, and through a good friend, George Gregory Smith, a resident of Florence, the Villa Quarto, an ancient home of royalty, on the hills west of Florence, was engaged. Smith wrote that it was a very beautiful place with a south-eastern exposure, looking out toward Valombrosa and the Chianti Hills. It had extensive grounds and stables, and the annual rental for it all was two thousand dollars a year. It seemed an ideal place, in prospect, and there was great hope that Mrs. Clemens would find her health once more in the Italian climate which she loved.

Perhaps at this point, when Mark Twain is once more leaving America, we may offer two letters from strangers to him—letters of appreciation—such as he was constantly receiving from those among the thousands to whom he had given happiness. The first is from Samuel Merwin, one day to become a popular novelist, then in the hour of his beginnings.

To Mark Twain, from Samuel Merwin:

PLAINFIELD, N. J.

August 4, 1903.

DEAR MR. CLEMENS,—For a good many years I have been struggling with the temptation to write you and thank you for the work you have done; and to-day I seem to be yielding.

During the past two years I have been reading through a group of writers who seem to me to represent about the best we have—Sir Thomas Malory, Spenser, Shakespeare, Boswell, Carlyle, Le Sage. In thinking over one and then another, and then all of them together, it was plain to see why they were great men and writers: each brought to his time some new blood, new ideas,—turned a new current into the stream. I suppose there have always been the careful, painstaking writers, the men who are always taken so seriously by their fellow craftsmen. It seems to be the unconventional man who is so rare—I mean the honestly unconventional man, who has to express himself in his own big way because the conventional way isn't big enough, because ne needs room and freedom.

We have a group of the more or less conventional men now—men of dignity and literary position. But in spite of their influence and of all the work they have done, there isn't one of them to whom one can give one's self up without reservation, not one whose ideas seem based on the deep foundation of all true philosophy,—except Mark Twain.

I hope this letter is not an impertinence. I have just been turning about, with my head full of Spenser and Shakespeare and "Gil Blas," looking for something in our own present day literature to which I could surrender myself as to those five gripping old writings. And nothing could I find until I took up "Life on the Mississippi," and "Huckleberry Finn," and, just now, the "Connecticut Yankee." It isn't the first time I have read any of these three, and it's because I know it won't be the last, because these books are the only ones written in my lifetime that claim my unreserved interest and admiration and, above all, my feelings, that I've felt I had to write this letter.

I like to think that "Tom Sawyer" and "Huckleberry Finn" will be looked upon, fifty or a hundred years from now, as the picture of buoyant, dramatic, human American life. I feel, deep in my own heart, pretty sure that they will be. They won't be looked on then as the work of a "humorist" any more than we think of Shakespeare as a humorist now. I don't mean by this to set up a comparison between Mark Twain and Shakespeare: I don't feel competent to do it; and I'm not at all sure that it could be done until Mark Twain's work shall have its fair share of historical perspective. But Shakespeare was a humorist and so, thank Heaven! is Mark Twain. And Shakespeare plunged deep into the deep, sad things of life; and so, in a different way (but in a way that has more than once brought tears to my eyes) has Mark Twain. But after all, it isn't because of any resemblance for anything that was ever before written that Mark Twain's books strike in so deep: it's rather because they've brought something really new into our literature—new, yet old as Adam and Eve and the Apple. And this achievement, the achievement of putting something into literature that was not there before, is, I should think, the most that any writer can ever hope to do. It is the one mark of distinction between the "lonesome" little group of big men and the vast herd of medium and small ones. Anyhow, this much I am sure of—to the young man who hopes, however feebly, to accomplish a little something, someday, as a writer, the one inspiring example of our time is Mark Twain. Very truly yours, SAMUEL MERWIN.

Mark Twain once said he could live a month on a good compliment, and from his reply, we may believe this one to belong in, that class.

To Samuel Merwin, in Plainfield, N. J.:

Aug. 16, '03.

DEAR MR. MERWIN,—What you have said has given me deep pleasure—indeed I think no words could be said that could give me more.

Very sincerely yours,

S. L. CLEMENS.

The next "compliment" is from one who remains unknown, for she failed to sign her name in full. But it is a lovely letter, and loses nothing by the fact that the writer of it was willing to remain in obscurity.

To Mark Twain, from Margaret M——:

PORTLAND, OREGON

Aug. 18, 1903.

MY DEAR, DEAR MARK TWAIN,—May a little girl write and tell you how dearly she loves and admires your writings? Well, I do and I want to tell you your ownself. Don't think me too impertinent for indeed I don't mean to be that! I have read everything of yours that I could get and parts that touch me I have read over and over again. They seem such dear friends to me, so like real live human beings talking and laughing, working and suffering too! One cannot but feel that it is your own life and experience that you have painted. So do not wonder that you seem a dear friend to me who has never even seen you. I often think of you as such in my own thoughts. I wonder if you will laugh when I tell you I have made a hero of you? For when people seem very sordid and mean and stupid (and it seems as if everybody was) then the thought will come like a little crumb of comfort "well, Mark Twain isn't anyway." And it does really brighten me up.

You see I have gotten an idea that you are a great, bright spirit of kindness and tenderness. One who can twist everybody's-even your own-faults and absurdities into hearty laughs. Even the person mocked must laugh! Oh, Dear! How often you have made me laugh! And yet as often you have struck something infinite away down deep in my heart so that I want to cry while half laughing!

So this all means that I want to thank you and to tell you. "God always love Mark Twain!" is often my wish. I dearly love to read books, and I never tire of reading yours; they always have a charm for me. Good-bye, I am afraid I have not expressed what I feel. But at least I have tried.

Sincerely yours.

MARGARET M.——

Clemens and family left Elmira October the 5th for New York City.

They remained at the Hotel Grosvenor until their sailing date,

October 24th. A few days earlier, Mr. Frank Doubleday sent a volume of Kipling's poems and de Blowitz's Memoirs for entertainment on the ship. Mark Twain's acknowledgment follows.

To F. N. Doubleday, in New York:

THE GROSVENOR,

October 12, '03.

DEAR DOUBLEDAY,—The books came—ever so many thanks. I have been reading "The Bell Buoy" and "The Old Men" over and over again—my custom with Kipling's work-and saving up the rest for other leisurely and luxurious meals. A bell-buoy is a deeply impressive fellow-being. In these many recent trips up and down the Sound in the Kanawha—[Mr. Rogers's yacht.]—he has talked to me nightly, sometimes in his pathetic and melancholy way, sometimes with his strenuous and urgent note, and I got his meaning—now I have his words! No one but Kipling could do this strong and vivid thing. Some day I hope to hear the poem chanted or sung—with the bell-buoy breaking in, out of the distance.

"The Old Men," delicious, isn't it? And so comically true. I haven't arrived there yet, but I suppose I am on the way....

Yours ever,

MARK.

P. S. Your letter has arrived. It makes me proud and glad—what Kipling says. I hope Fate will fetch him to Florence while we are there. I would rather see him than any other man.

We've let the Tarrytown house for a year. Man, you would never have believed a person could let a house in these times. That one's for sale, the Hartford one is sold. When we buy again may we—may I—be damned....

I've dipped into Blowitz and find him quaintly and curiously interesting. I think he tells the straight truth, too. I knew him a little, 23 years ago.

The appreciative word which Kipling had sent Doubleday was: "I love to think of the great and God-like Clemens. He is the biggest man you have on your side of the water by a damn sight, and don't you forget it. Cervantes was a relation of his."

XLIII. LETTERS OF 1904. TO VARIOUS PERSONS. LIFE IN VILLA QUARTO. DEATH OF MRS. CLEMENS. THE RETURN TO AMERICA.

Mrs. Clemens stood the voyage to Italy very well and, in due time, the family were installed in the Villa Reale di Quarto, the picturesque old Palace of Cosimo, a spacious, luxurious place, even if not entirely cheerful or always comfortable during the changeable Tuscan winter. Congratulated in a letter from MacAlister in being in the midst of Florentine sunshine, he answered: "Florentine sunshine? Bless you, there isn't any. We have heavy fogs every morning, and rain all day. This house is not merely large, it is vast—therefore I think it must always lack the home feeling."

Neither was their landlady, the American wife of an Italian count, all that could be desired. From a letter to Twichell, however, we learn that Mark Twain's work was progressing well.

To Rev. J. H. Twichell, in Hartford:

VILLA DI QUARTO,

FLORENCE, Jan. 7, '04.

DEAR JOE,—... I have had a handsome success, in one way, here. I left

New York under a sort of half promise to furnish to the Harper magazines 30,000 words this year. Magazining is difficult work because every third page represents 2 pages that you have put in the fire; (because you are nearly sure to start wrong twice) and so when you have finished an article and are willing to let it go to print it represents only 10 cents a word instead of 30.

But this time I had the curious (and unprecedented) luck to start right in each case. I turned out 37,000 words in 25 working days; and the reason I think I started right every time is, that not only have I approved and accepted the several articles, but the court of last resort (Livy) has done the same.

On many of the between-days I did some work, but only of an idle and not necessarily necessary sort, since it will not see print until I am dead. I shall continue this (an hour per day) but the rest of the year I expect to put in on a couple of long books (half-completed ones.) No more magazine-work hanging over my head.

This secluded and silent solitude this clean, soft air and this enchanting view of Florence, the great valley and the snow-mountains that frame it are the right conditions for work. They are a persistent inspiration. To-day is very lovely; when the afternoon arrives there will be a new picture every hour till dark, and each of them divine—or progressing from divine to diviner and divinest. On this (second) floor Clara's room commands the finest; she keeps a window ten feet high wide open all the time and frames it in. I go in from time to time, every day and trade sass for a look. The central detail is a distant and stately snow-hump that rises above and behind blackforested hills, and its sloping vast buttresses, velvety and sun-polished with purple shadows between, make the sort of picture we knew that time we walked in Switzerland in the days of our youth.

I wish I could show your letter to Livy—but she must wait a week or so for it. I think I told you she had a prostrating week of tonsillitis a month ago; she has remained very feeble ever since, and confined to the bed of course, but we allow ourselves to believe she will regain the lost ground in another month. Her physician is Professor Grocco—she could not have a better. And she has a very good trained nurse.

Love to all of you from all of us. And to all of our dear Hartford friends.

MARK

P. S. 3 days later.

Livy is as remarkable as ever. The day I wrote you—that night, I mean—she had a bitter attack of gout or rheumatism occupying the whole left arm from shoulder to fingers, accompanied by fever. The pains racked her 50 or 60 hours; they have departed, now—and already she is planning a trip to Egypt next fall, and a winter's sojourn there! This is life in her yet.

You will be surprised that I was willing to do so much magazine-writing—a thing I have always been chary about—but I had good reasons. Our expenses have been so prodigious for a year and a half, and are still so prodigious, that Livy was worrying altogether too much about them, and doing a very dangerous amount of lying awake on their account. It was necessary to stop that, and it is now stopped.

Yes, she is remarkable, Joe. Her rheumatic attack set me to cursing and swearing, without limit as to time or energy, but it merely concentrated her patience and her unconquerable fortitude. It is the difference between us. I can't count the different kinds of ailments which have assaulted her in this fiendish year and a half—and I forgive none of them—but here she comes up again as bright and fresh and enterprising as ever, and goes to planning about Egypt, with a hope and a confidence which are to me amazing.

Clara is calling for me—we have to go into town and pay calls.

MARK.

In Florence, that winter, Clemens began dictating to his secretary some autobiographical chapters. This was the work which was "not to see print until I am dead." He found it a pleasant, lazy occupation and wrote his delight in it to Howells in a letter which seems not to have survived. In his reply, Howells wrote: "You do stir me mightily with the hope of dictating and I will try it when I get the chance. But there is the tempermental difference. You are dramatic and unconscious; you count the thing more than yourself; I am cursed with consciousness to the core, and can't say myself out; I am always saying myself in, and setting myself above all that I say, as of more worth. Lately I have felt as if I were rotting with egotism. I don't admire myself; I am sick of myself; but I can't think of anything else. Here I am at it now, when I ought to be rejoicing with you at the blessing you have found.... I'd like, immensely, to read your autobiography. You always rather bewildered me by your veracity, and I fancy you may tell the truth about yourself. But all of it? The black truth which we all know of ourselves in our hearts, or only the whity-brown truth of the pericardium, or the nice, whitened truth of the shirtfront? Even you won't tell the black heart's—truth. The man who could do it would be famed to the last day the sun shone upon."

We gather from Mark Twain's answer that he was not deceiving himself in the matter of his confessions.

To W. D. Howells, in New York:

VILLA DI QUARTO, FLORENCE,

March 14, '04.

DEAR HOWELLS,—Yes, I set up the safeguards, in the first day's dictating; taking this position: that an autobiography is the truest of all books; for while it inevitably consists mainly of extinctions of the truth, shirkings of the truth, partial revealments of the truth, with hardly an instance of plain straight truth, the remorseless truth is there, between the lines, where the author is raking dust upon it, the result being that the reader knows the author in spite of his wily diligences.

The summer in England! you can't ask better luck than that. Then you will run over to Florence; we shall all be hungry to see you-all. We are hunting for another villa, (this one is plenty large enough but has no room in it) but even if we find it I am afraid it will be months before we can move Mrs. Clemens. Of course it will. But it comforts us to let on that we think otherwise, and these pretensions help to keep hope alive in her.

Good-bye, with love, Amen.

Yours ever

MARK.

News came of the death of Henry M. Stanley, one of Mark Twain's oldest friends. Clemens once said that he had met Stanley in St. Louis where he (Clemens) had delivered a lecture which Stanley had reported. In the following letter he fixes the date of their meeting as early in 1867, which would be immediately after Mark Twain's return from California, and just prior to the Quaker City excursion—a fact which is interesting only because it places the two men together when each was at the very beginning of a great career.

To Lady Stanley, in England:

VILLA DI QUARTO, FIRENZE, May 11, '04.

DEAR LADY STANLEY,—I have lost a dear and honored friend—how fast they fall about me now, in my age! The world has lost a tried and proved hero. And you—what have you lost? It is beyond estimate—we who know you, and what he was to you, know that. How far he stretches across my life! I knew him when his work was all before him five years before the great day that he wrote his name far-away up on the blue of the sky for the world to see and applaud and remember; I have known him as friend and intimate ever since. It is 37 years. I have known no other friend and intimate so long, except John Hay—a friendship which dates from the same year and the same half of it, the first half of 1867. I grieve with you and with your family, dear Lady Stanley, it is all I can do; but that I do out of my heart. It would be we, instead of I, if Mrs. Clemens knew, but in all these 20 months that she has lain a prisoner in her bed we have hidden from her all things that could sadden her. Many a friend is gone whom she still asks about and still thinks is living.

In deepest sympathy I beg the privilege of signing myself

Your friend,

S. L. CLEMENS.

To Rev. J. H. Twichell, in Hartford:

VILLA DI QUARTO, May 11, '04

DEAR JOE,—Yours has this moment arrived—just as I was finishing a note to poor Lady Stanley. I believe the last country-house visit we paid in England was to Stanley's. Lord, how my friends and acquaintances fall about me now, in my gray-headed days! Vereschagin, Mommsen, Dvorak, Lenbach, Jokai—all so recently, and now Stanley. I had known Stanley 37 years. Goodness, who is it I haven't known! As a rule the necrologies find me personally interested—when they treat of old stagers. Generally when a man dies who is worth cabling, it happens that I have run across him somewhere, some time or other.

Oh, say! Down by the Laurentian Library there's a marble image that has been sitting on its pedestal some 450 Years, if my dates are right—Cosimo I.

I've seen the back of it many a time, but not the front; but yesterday I twisted my head around after we had driven by, and the profane exclamation burst from my mouth before I could think: "there's Chauncey Depew!"

I mean to get a photo of it—and use it if it confirms yesterday's conviction. That's a very nice word from the Catholic Magazine and I am glad you sent it. I mean to show it to my priest—we are very fond of him. He is a stealing man, and is also learnedly scientific. He invented the thing which records the seismatic disturbances, for the peoples of the earth. And he's an astronomer and has an observatory of his own.

Ah, many's the cry I have, over reflecting that maybe we could have had Young Harmony for Livy, and didn't have wit enough to think of it.

Speaking of Livy reminds me that your inquiry arrives at a good time (unberufen) It has been weeks (I don't know how many!) since we could have said a hopeful word, but this morning Katy came the minute the day-nurse came on watch and said words of a strange and long-forgotten sound: "Mr. Clemens, Mrs. Clemens is really and truly better!—anybody can see it; she sees it herself; and last night at 9 o'clock she said it."

There—it is heart-warming, it is splendid, it is sublime; let us enjoy it, let us make the most of it today—and bet not a farthing on tomorrow. The tomorrows have nothing for us. Too many times they have breathed the word of promise to our ear and broken it to our hope. We take no tomorrow's word any more.

You've done a wonder, Joe: you've written a letter that can be sent in to Livy—that doesn't often happen, when either a friend or a stranger writes. You did whirl in a P. S. that wouldn't do, but you wrote it on a margin of a page in such a way that I was able to clip off the margin clear across both pages, and now Livy won't perceive that the sheet isn't the same size it used to was. It was about Aldrich's son, and I came near forgetting to remove it. It should have been written on a loose strip and enclosed. That son died on the 5th of March and Aldrich wrote me on the night before that his minutes were numbered. On the 18th Livy asked after that patient, and I was prepared, and able to give her a grateful surprise by telling her "the Aldriches are no longer uneasy about him."

I do wish I could have been present and heard Charley Clark. When he can't light up a dark place nobody can.

With lots of love to you all.

MARK.

Mrs. Clemens had her bad days and her good days-days when there seemed no ray of light, and others that seemed almost to promise recovery. The foregoing letter to Twichell, and the one which follows, to Richard Watson Gilder, reflect the hope and fear that daily and hourly alternated at Villa Quarto

To Richard Watson Gilder, in New York:

VILLA DI QUARTO, FLORENCE,

May 12, '04.

DEAR GILDER,—A friend of ours (the Baroness de Nolda) was here this afternoon and wanted a note of introduction to the Century, for she has something to sell to you in case you'll want to make her an offer after seeing a sample of the goods. I said "With pleasure: get the goods ready, send the same to me, I will have Jean type-write them, then I will mail them to the Century and tonight I will write the note to Mr. Gilder and start it along. Also write me a letter embodying what you have been saying to me about the goods and your proposed plan of arranging and explaining them, and I will forward that to Gilder too."

As to the Baroness. She is a German; 30 years old; was married at 17; is very pretty-indeed I might say very pretty; has a lot of sons (5) running up from seven to 12 years old. Her husband is a Russian. They live half the time in Russia and the other half in Florence, and supply population alternately to the one country and then to the other. Of course it is a family that speaks languages. This occurs at their table—I know it by experience: It is Babel come again. The other day, when no guests were present to keep order, the tribes were all talking at once, and 6 languages were being traded in; at last the littlest boy lost his temper and screamed out at the top of his voice, with angry sobs: "Mais, vraiment, io non capisco gar nichts."

The Baroness is a little afraid of her English, therefore she will write her remarks in French—I said there's a plenty of translators in New York. Examine her samples and drop her a line.

For two entire days, now, we have not been anxious about Mrs. Clemens (unberufen). After 20 months of bed-ridden solitude and bodily misery she all of a sudden ceases to be a pallid shrunken shadow, and looks bright and young and pretty. She remains what she always was, the most wonderful creature of fortitude, patience, endurance and recuperative power that ever was. But ah, dear, it won't last; this fiendish malady will play new treacheries upon her, and I shall go back to my prayers again—unutterable from any pulpit!

With love to you and yours,

S. L. C.

May 13 10 A.M. I have just paid one of my pair of permitted 2 minutes visits per day to the sick room. And found what I have learned to expect—retrogression, and that pathetic something in the eye which betrays the secret of a waning hope.

The year of the World's Fair had come, and an invitation from Gov. Francis, of Missouri, came to Mark Twain in Florence, personally inviting him to attend the great celebration and carry off first prize. We may believe that Clemens felt little in the spirit of humor, but to such an invitation he must send a cheerful, even if disappointing, answer.

To Gov. Francis, of Missouri:

VILLA DI QUARTO, FIRENZE,

May 26, 1904.

DEAR GOVERNOR FRANCIS,—It has been a dear wish of mine to exhibit myself at the Great Fair and get a prize, but circumstances beyond my control have interfered, and I must remain in Florence. Although I have never taken prizes anywhere else I used to take them at school in Missouri half a century ago, and I ought to be able to repeat, now, if I could have a chance. I used to get the medal for good spelling, every week, and I could have had the medal for good conduct if there hadn't been so much corruption in Missouri in those days; still, I got it several times by trading medals and giving boot. I am willing to give boot now, if—however, those days are forever gone by in Missouri, and perhaps it is better so. Nothing ever stops the way it was in this changeable world. Although I cannot be at the Fair, I am going to be represented there anyway, by a portrait, by Professor Gelli. You will find it excellent. Good judges here say it is better than the original. They say it has all the merits of the original and keeps still, besides. It sounds like flattery, but it is just true.

I suppose you will get a prize, because you have created the most prodigious and in all ways most wonderful Fair the planet has ever seen. Very well, you have indeed earned it: and with it the gratitude of the State and the nation.

Sincerely yours,

MARK TWAIN

It was only a few days after the foregoing was written that death entered Villa Quarto—unexpectedly at last—for with the first June days Mrs. Clemens had seemed really to improve. It was on Sunday, June 5th, that the end came. Clemens, with his daughter Jean, had returned from a long drive, during which they had visited a Villa with the thought of purchase. On their return they were told that their patient had been better that afternoon than for three months. Yet it was only a few hours later that she left them, so suddenly and quietly that even those near her did not at first realize that she was gone.

To W. D. Howells, in New York.

VILLA DI QUARTO, FLORENCE,

June 6, '94.

DEAR HOWELLS,—Last night at 9.20 I entered Mrs. Clemens's room to say the usual goodnight—and she was dead—tho' no one knew it. She had been cheerfully talking, a moment before. She was sitting up in bed—she had not lain down for months—and Katie and the nurse were supporting her. They supposed she had fainted, and they were holding the oxygen pipe to her mouth, expecting to revive her. I bent over her and looked in her face, and I think I spoke—I was surprised and troubled that she did not notice me. Then we understood, and our hearts broke. How poor we are today!

But how thankful I am that her persecutions are ended. I would not call her back if I could.

Today, treasured in her worn old Testament, I found a dear and gentle letter from you, dated Far Rockaway, Sept. 13, 1896, about our poor Susy's death. I am tired and old; I wish I were with Livy.

I send my love-and hers-to you all.

S. L. C.

In a letter to Twichell he wrote: "How sweet she was in death; how young, how beautiful, how like her dear, girlish self cf thirty years ago; not a gray hair showing."

The family was now without plans for the future until they remembered the summer home of R. W. Gilder, at Tyringham, Massachusetts, and the possibility of finding lodgment for themselves in that secluded corner of New England. Clemens wrote without delay, as follows:

To R. W. Gilder, in New York:

VILLA DI QUARTO, FLORENCE,

June 7, '04.

DEAR GILDER FAMILY,—I have been worrying and worrying to know what to do: at last I went to the girls with an idea: to ask the Gilders to get us shelter near their summer home. It was the first time they have not shaken their heads. So to-morrow I will cable to you and shall hope to be in time.

An hour ago the best heart that ever beat for me and mine went silent out of this house, and I am as one who wanders and has lost his way. She who is gone was our head, she was our hands. We are now trying to make plans—we: we who have never made a plan before, nor ever needed to. If she could speak to us she would make it all simple and easy with a word, and our perplexities would vanish away. If she had known she was near to death she would have told us where to go and what to do: but she was not suspecting, neither were we. (She had been chatting cheerfully a moment before, and in an instant she was gone from us and we did not know it. We were not alarmed, we did not know anything had happened. It was a blessed death—she passed away without knowing it.) She was all our riches and she is gone: she was our breath, she was our life and now we are nothing.

We send you our love—and with it the love of you that was in her heart when she died.

S. L. CLEMENS.

Howells wrote his words of sympathy, adding: "The character which now remains a memory was one of the most perfect ever formed on the earth," and again, after having received Clemens's letter: "I cannot speak of your wife's having kept that letter of mine where she did. You know how it must humiliate a man in his unworthiness to have anything of his so consecrated. She hallowed what she touched, far beyond priests."

To W. D. Howells, in New York:

VILLA DI QUARTO, '04.

June 12, 6 p. m.

DEAR HOWELLS,—We have to sit and hold our hands and wait—in the silence and solitude of this prodigious house; wait until June 25, then we go to Naples and sail in the Prince Oscar the 26th. There is a ship 12 days earlier (but we came in that one.) I see Clara twice a day—morning and evening—greeting—nothing more is allowed. She keeps her bed, and says nothing. She has not cried yet. I wish she could cry. It would break Livy's heart to see Clara. We excuse ourselves from all the friends that call—though of course only intimates come. Intimates—but they are not the old old friends, the friends of the old, old times when we laughed.

Shall we ever laugh again? If I could only see a dog that I knew in the old times! and could put my arms around his neck and tell him all, everything, and ease my heart.

Think—in 3 hours it will be a week!—and soon a month; and by and by a year. How fast our dead fly from us.

She loved you so, and was always as pleased as a child with any notice you took of her.

Soon your wife will be with you, oh fortunate man! And John, whom mine was so fond of. The sight of him was such a delight to her. Lord, the old friends, how dear they are.

S. L. C.

To Rev. J. R. Twichell, in Hartford:

VILLA DI QUARTO, FLORENCE,

June 18, '04.

DEAR JOE,—It is 13 days. I am bewildered and must remain so for a time longer. It was so sudden, so unexpected. Imagine a man worth a hundred millions who finds himself suddenly penniless and fifty million in debt in his old age.

I was richer than any other person in the world, and now I am that pauper without peer. Some day I will tell you about it, not now.

MARK.

A tide of condolence flowed in from all parts of the world. It was impossible to answer all. Only a few who had been their closest friends received a written line, but the little printed acknowledgment which was returned was no mere formality. It was a heartfelt, personal word.

They arrived in America in July, and were accompanied by Twichell to Elmira, and on the 14th Mrs. Clemens was laid to rest by the side of Susy and little Langdon. R. W. Gilder had arranged for them to occupy, for the summer, a cottage on his place at Tyringham, in the Berkshire Hills. By November they were at the Grosvenor, in New York, preparing to establish themselves in a house which they had taken on the corner of Ninth Street and Fifth Avenue—Number 21.

To F. N. Doubleday, in New York:

DEAR DOUBLEDAY,—I did not know you were going to England: I would have freighted you with such messages of homage and affection to Kipling. And I would have pressed his hand, through you, for his sympathy with me in my crushing loss, as expressed by him in his letter to Gilder. You know my feeling for Kipling and that it antedates that expression.

I was glad that the boys came here to invite me to the house-warming and I think they understood why a man in the shadow of a calamity like mine could not go.

It has taken three months to repair and renovate our house—corner of 9th and 5th Avenue, but I shall be in it in io or 15 days hence. Much of the furniture went into it today (from Hartford). We have not seen it for 13 years. Katy Leary, our old housekeeper, who has been in our service more than 24 years, cried when she told me about it to-day. She said "I had forgotten it was so beautiful, and it brought Mrs. Clemens right back to me—in that old time when she was so young and lovely."

Jean and my secretary and the servants whom we brought from Italy because Mrs. Clemens liked them so well, are still keeping house in the Berkshire hills—and waiting. Clara (nervously wrecked by her mother's death) is in the hands of a specialist in 69th St., and I shall not be allowed to have any communication with her—even telephone—for a year. I am in this comfortable little hotel, and still in bed—for I dasn't budge till I'm safe from my pet devil, bronchitis.

Isn't it pathetic? One hour and ten minutes before Mrs. Clemens died I was saying to her "To-day, after five months search, I've found the villa that will content you: to-morrow you will examine the plans and give it your consent and I will buy it." Her eyes danced with pleasure, for she longed for a home of her own. And there, on that morrow, she lay white and cold. And unresponsive to my reverent caresses—a new thing to me and a new thing to her; that had not happened before in five and thirty years.

I am coming to see you and Mrs. Doubleday by and bye. She loved and honored Mrs. Doubleday and her work.

Always yours,

MARK.

It was a presidential year and the air was thick with politics. Mark Twain was no longer actively interested in the political situation; he was only disheartened by the hollowness and pretense of office-seeking, and the methods of office-seekers in general. Grieved that Twichell should still pin his faith to any party when all parties were so obviously venal and time-serving, he wrote in outspoken and rather somber protest.

To Rev. J. H. Twichell, in Hartford:

THE GROSVENOR, Nov. 4, '04.

Oh, dear! get out of that sewer—party politics—dear Joe. At least with your mouth. We hail only two men who could make speeches for their parties and preserve their honor and their dignity. One of them is dead. Possibly there were four. I am sorry for John Hay; sorry and ashamed. And yet I know he couldn't help it. He wears the collar, and he had to pay the penalty. Certainly he had no more desire to stand up before a mob of confiding human incapables and debauch them than you had. Certainly he took no more real pleasure in distorting history, concealing facts, propagating immoralities, and appealing to the sordid side of human nature than did you; but he was his party's property, and he had to climb away down and do it.

It is interesting, wonderfully interesting—the miracles which party-politics can do with a man's mental and moral make-up. Look at McKinley, Roosevelt, and yourself: in private life spotless in character; honorable, honest, just, humane, generous; scorning trickeries, treacheries, suppressions of the truth, mistranslations of the meanings of facts, the filching of credit earned by another, the condoning of crime, the glorifying of base acts: in public political life the reverse of all this.

McKinley was a silverite—you concealed it. Roosevelt was a silverite—you concealed it. Parker was a silverite—you publish it. Along with a shudder and a warning: "He was unsafe then. Is he any safer now?"

Joe, even I could be guilty of such a thing as that—if I were in party-politics; I really believe it.

Mr. Cleveland gave the country the gold standard; by implication you credit the matter to the Republican party.

By implication you prove the whole annual pension-scoop, concealing the fact that the bulk of the money goes to people who in no way deserve it. You imply that all the batteners upon this bribery-fund are Republicans. An indiscreet confession, since about half of them must have been Democrats before they were bought.

You as good as praise Order 78. It is true you do not shout, and you do not linger, you only whisper and skip—still, what little you do in the matter is complimentary to the crime.

It means, if it means anything, that our outlying properties will all be given up by the Democrats, and our flag hauled down. All of them? Not only the properties stolen by Mr. McKinley and Mr. Roosevelt, but the properties honestly acquired? Joe, did you believe that hardy statement when you made it? Yet you made it, and there it stands in permanent print. Now what moral law would suffer if we should give up the stolen ones? But—

"You know our standard-bearer. He will maintain all that we have gained"—by whatever process. Land, I believe you!

By George, Joe, you are as handy at the game as if you had been in training for it all your life. Your campaign Address is built from the ground up upon the oldest and best models. There isn't a paragraph in it whose facts or morals will wash—not even a sentence, I believe.

But you will soon be out of this. You didn't want to do it—that is sufficiently apparent, thanks be!—but you couldn't well get out of it. In a few days you will be out of it, and then you can fumigate yourself and take up your legitimate work again and resume your clean and wholesome private character once more and be happy—and useful.

I know I ought to hand you some guff, now, as propitiation and apology for these reproaches, but on the whole I believe I won't.

I have inquired, and find that Mitsikuri does not arrive here until to-morrow night. I shall watch out, and telephone again, for I greatly want to see him.

Always Yours,

MARK.

P. S.—Nov, 4. I wish I could learn to remember that it is unjust and dishonorable to put blame upon the human race for any of its acts. For it did not make itself, it did not make its nature, it is merely a machine, it is moved wholly by outside influences, it has no hand in creating the outside influences nor in choosing which of them it will welcome or reject, its performance is wholly automatic, it has no more mastership nor authority over its mind than it has over its stomach, which receives material from the outside and does as it pleases with it, indifferent to it's proprietor's suggestions, even, let alone his commands; wherefore, whatever the machine does—so called crimes and infamies included—is the personal act of its Maker, and He, solely, is responsible. I wish I could learn to pity the human race instead of censuring it and laughing at it; and I could, if the outside influences of old habit were not so strong upon my machine. It vexes me to catch myself praising the clean private citizen Roosevelt, and blaming the soiled President Roosevelt, when I know that neither praise nor blame is due to him for any thought or word or deed of his, he being merely a helpless and irresponsible coffee-mill ground by the hand of God.

Through a misunderstanding, Clemens, something more than a year earlier, had severed his connection with the Players' Club, of which he had been one of the charter members. Now, upon his return to New York, a number of his friends joined in an invitation to him to return. It was not exactly a letter they sent, but a bit of an old Scotch song—

"To Mark Twain

from

The Clansmen.

Will ye no come back again,
Will ye no come back again?
Better lo'ed ye canna be.
Will ye no come back again?"

Those who signed it were David Monroe, of the North American Review; Robert Reid, the painter, and about thirty others of the Round Table Group, so called because its members were accustomed to lunching at a large round table in a bay window of the Player dining-room. Mark Twain's reply was prompt and heartfelt. He wrote:

To Robt. Reid and the Others:

WELL-BELOVED,—Surely those lovely verses went to Prince Charley's heart, if he had one, and certainly they have gone to mine. I shall be glad and proud to come back again after such a moving and beautiful compliment as this from comrades whom I have loved so long. I hope you can poll the necessary vote; I know you will try, at any rate. It will be many months before I can foregather with you, for this black border is not perfunctory, not a convention; it symbolizes the loss of one whose memory is the only thing I worship.

It is not necessary for me to thank you—and words could not deliver what I feel, anyway. I will put the contents of your envelope in the small casket where I keep the things which have become sacred to me.

S. L. C.

A year later, Mark Twain did "come back again," as an honorary life member, and was given a dinner of welcome by those who had signed the lines urging his return.

XLIV. LETTERS OF 1905. TO TWICHELL, MR. DUNEKA AND OTHERS. POLITICS AND HUMANITY. A SUMMER AT DUBLIN. MARK TWAIN AT 70.

In 1884 Mark Twain had abandoned the Republican Party to vote for Cleveland. He believed the party had become corrupt, and to his last day it was hard for him to see anything good in Republican policies or performance. He was a personal friend of Theodore Roosevelt's but, as we have seen in a former letter, Roosevelt the politician rarely found favor in his eyes. With or without justification, most of the President's political acts invited his caustic sarcasm and unsparing condemnation. Another letter to Twichell of this time affords a fair example.

To Rev. J. H. Twichell, in Hartford:

Feb. 16, '05.

DEAR JOE,—I knew I had in me somewhere a definite feeling about the President if I could only find the words to define it with. Here they are, to a hair—from Leonard Jerome: "For twenty years I have loved Roosevelt the man and hated Roosevelt the statesman and politician."

It's mighty good. Every time, in 25 years, that I have met Roosevelt the man, a wave of welcome has streaked through me with the hand-grip; but whenever (as a rule) I meet Roosevelt the statesman and politician, I find him destitute of morals and not respectworthy. It is plain that where his political self and his party self are concerned he has nothing resembling a conscience; that under those inspirations he is naively indifferent to the restraints of duty and even unaware of them; ready to kick the Constitution into the back yard whenever it gets in the way; and whenever he smells a vote, not only willing but eager to buy it, give extravagant rates for it and pay the bill not out of his own pocket or the party's, but out of the nation's, by cold pillage. As per Order 78 and the appropriation of the Indian trust funds.

But Roosevelt is excusable—I recognize it and (ought to) concede it. We are all insane, each in his own way, and with insanity goes irresponsibility. Theodore the man is sane; in fairness we ought to keep in mind that Theodore, as statesman and politician, is insane and irresponsible.

Do not throw these enlightenments aside, but study them, let them raise you to higher planes and make you better. You taught me in my callow days, let me pay back the debt now in my old age out of a thesaurus with wisdom smelted from the golden ores of experience.

Ever yours for sweetness and light

MARK.

The next letter to Twichell takes up politics and humanity in general, in a manner complimentary to neither. Mark Twain was never really a pessimist, but he had pessimistic intervals, such as come to most of us in life's later years, and at such times he let himself go without stint concerning "the damned human race," as he called it, usually with a manifest sense of indignation that he should be a member of it. In much of his later writing —A Mysterious Stranger for example—he said his say with but small restraint, and certainly in his purely intellectual moments he was likely to be a pessimist of the most extreme type, capably damning the race and the inventor of it. Yet, at heart, no man loved his kind more genuinely, or with deeper compassion, than Mark Twain, perhaps for its very weaknesses. It was only that he had intervals —frequent intervals, and rather long ones—when he did not admire it, and was still more doubtful as to the ways of providence.

To Rev. J. H. Twichell, in Hartford:

March 14, '05.

DEAR JOE,—I have a Puddn'head maxim:

"When a man is a pessimist before 48 he knows too much; if he is an optimist after it, he knows too little."

It is with contentment, therefore, that I reflect that I am better and wiser than you. Joe, you seem to be dealing in "bulks," now; the "bulk" of the farmers and U. S. Senators are "honest." As regards purchase and sale with money? Who doubts it? Is that the only measure of honesty? Aren't there a dozen kinds of honesty which can't be measured by the money-standard? Treason is treason—and there's more than one form of it; the money-form is but one of them. When a person is disloyal to any confessed duty, he is plainly and simply dishonest, and knows it; knows it, and is privately troubled about it and not proud of himself. Judged by this standard—and who will challenge the validity of it?—there isn't an honest man in Connecticut, nor in the Senate, nor anywhere else. I do not even except myself, this time.

Am I finding fault with you and the rest of the populace? No—I assure you I am not. For I know the human race's limitations, and this makes it my duty—my pleasant duty—to be fair to it. Each person in it is honest in one or several ways, but no member of it is honest in all the ways required by—by what? By his own standard. Outside of that, as I look at it, there is no obligation upon him.

Am I honest? I give you my word of honor (private) I am not. For seven years I have suppressed a book which my conscience tells me I ought to publish. I hold it a duty to publish it. There are other difficult duties which I am equal to, but I am not equal to that one. Yes, even I am dishonest. Not in many ways, but in some. Forty-one, I think it is. We are certainly all honest in one or several ways—every man in the world—though I have reason to think I am the only one whose black-list runs so light. Sometimes I feel lonely enough in this lofty solitude.

Yes, oh, yes, I am not overlooking the "steady progress from age to age of the coming of the kingdom of God and righteousness." "From age to age"—yes, it describes that giddy gait. I (and the rocks) will not live to see it arrive, but that is all right—it will arrive, it surely will. But you ought not to be always ironically apologizing for the Deity. If that thing is going to arrive, it is inferable that He wants it to arrive; and so it is not quite kind of you, and it hurts me, to see you flinging sarcasms at the gait of it. And yet it would not be fair in me not to admit that the sarcasms are deserved. When the Deity wants a thing, and after working at it for "ages and ages" can't show even a shade of progress toward its accomplishment, we—well, we don't laugh, but it is only because we dasn't. The source of "righteousness"—is in the heart? Yes. And engineered and directed by the brain? Yes. Well, history and tradition testify that the heart is just about what it was in the beginning; it has undergone no shade of change. Its good and evil impulses and their consequences are the same today that they were in Old Bible times, in Egyptian times, in Greek times, in Middle Age times, in Twentieth Century times. There has been no change.

Meantime, the brain has undergone no change. It is what it always was. There are a few good brains and a multitude of poor ones. It was so in Old Bible times and in all other times—Greek, Roman, Middle Ages and Twentieth Century. Among the savages—all the savages—the average brain is as competent as the average brain here or elsewhere. I will prove it to you, some time, if you like. And there are great brains among them, too. I will prove that also, if you like.

Well, the 19th century made progress—the first progress after "ages and ages"—colossal progress. In what? Materialities. Prodigious acquisitions were made in things which add to the comfort of many and make life harder for as many more. But the addition to righteousness? Is that discoverable? I think not. The materialities were not invented in the interest of righteousness; that there is more righteousness in the world because of them than there, was before, is hardly demonstrable, I think. In Europe and America, there is a vast change (due to them) in ideals—do you admire it? All Europe and all America, are feverishly scrambling for money. Money is the supreme ideal—all others take tenth place with the great bulk of the nations named. Money-lust has always existed, but not in the history of the world was it ever a craze, a madness, until your time and mine. This lust has rotted these nations; it has made them hard, sordid, ungentle, dishonest, oppressive.

Did England rise against the infamy of the Boer war? No—rose in favor of it. Did America rise against the infamy of the Phillipine war? No—rose in favor of it. Did Russia rise against the infamy of the present war? No—sat still and said nothing. Has the Kingdom of God advanced in Russia since the beginning of time?

Or in Europe and America, considering the vast backward step of the money-lust? Or anywhere else? If there has been any progress toward righteousness since the early days of Creation—which, in my ineradicable honesty, I am obliged to doubt—I think we must confine it to ten per cent of the populations of Christendom, (but leaving, Russia, Spain and South America entirely out.) This gives us 320,000,000 to draw the ten per cent from. That is to say, 32,000,000 have advanced toward righteousness and the Kingdom of God since the "ages and ages" have been flying along, the Deity sitting up there admiring. Well, you see it leaves 1,200,000,000 out of the race. They stand just where they have always stood; there has been no change.

N. B. No charge for these informations. Do come down soon, Joe.

With love,

MARK.

St. Clair McKelway, of The Brooklyn Eagle, narrowly escaped injuries in a railway accident, and received the following. Clemens and McKelway were old friends.

To St. Clair McKelway, in Brooklyn:

21 FIFTH AVE. Sunday Morning.

April 30, 1905.

DEAR McKELWAY, Your innumerable friends are grateful, most grateful.

As I understand the telegrams, the engineer of your train had never seen a locomotive before. Very well, then, I am once more glad that there is an Ever-watchful Providence to foresee possible results and send Ogdens and McIntyres along to save our friends.

The Government's Official report, showing that our railways killed twelve hundred persons last year and injured sixty thousand convinces me that under present conditions one Providence is not enough to properly and efficiently take care of our railroad business. But it is characteristically American—always trying to get along short-handed and save wages.

I am helping your family congratulate themselves, and am your friend as always.

S. L. CLEMENS.

Clemens did not spend any more summers at Quarry Farm. All its associations were beautiful and tender, but they could only sadden him. The life there had been as of another world, sunlit, idyllic, now forever vanished. For the summer of 1905 he leased the Copley Green house at Dublin, New Hampshire, where there was a Boston colony of writing and artistic folk, including many of his long-time friends. Among them was Colonel Thomas Wentworth Higginson, who wrote a hearty letter of welcome when he heard the news. Clemens replied in kind.

To Col. Thomas Wentworth Higginson, in Boston:

21 FIFTH AVE. Sunday, March 26, 1905.

DEAR COL. HIGGINSON,—I early learned that you would be my neighbor in the Summer and I rejoiced, recognizing in you and your family a large asset. I hope for frequent intercourse between the two households. I shall have my youngest daughter with me. The other one will go from the rest-cure in this city to the rest-cure in Norfolk Conn and we shall not see her before autumn. We have not seen her since the middle of October.

Jean (the youngest daughter) went to Dublin and saw the house and came back charmed with it. I know the Thayers of old—manifestly there is no lack of attractions up there. Mrs. Thayer and I were shipmates in a wild excursion perilously near 40 years ago.

You say you "send with this" the story. Then it should be here but it isn't, when I send a thing with another thing, the other thing goes but the thing doesn't, I find it later—still on the premises. Will you look it up now and send it?

Aldrich was here half an hour ago, like a breeze from over the fields, with the fragrance still upon his spirit. I am tired of waiting for that man to get old.

Sincerely yours,

S. L. C.

Mark Twain was in his seventieth year, old neither in mind nor body, but willing to take life more quietly, to refrain from travel and gay events. A sort of pioneers' reunion was to be held on the Pacific Coast, and a letter from Robert Fulton, of Reno, Nevada, invited Clemens to attend. He did not go, but he sent a letter that we may believe was the next best thing to those who heard it read.

To Robert Fulton, in Reno, Nevada:

IN THE MOUNTAINS,

May 24, 1905.

DEAR MR. FULTON,—I remember, as if it were yesterday, that when I disembarked from the overland stage in front of the Ormsby in Carson City in August, 1861, I was not expecting to be asked to come again. I was tired, discouraged, white with alkali dust, and did not know anybody; and if you had said then, "Cheer up, desolate stranger, don't be down-hearted—pass on, and come again in 1905," you cannot think how grateful I would have been and how gladly I would have closed the contract. Although I was not expecting to be invited, I was watching out for it, and was hurt and disappointed when you started to ask me and changed it to, "How soon are you going away?"

But you have made it all right, now, the wound is closed. And so I thank you sincerely for the invitation; and with you, all Reno, and if I were a few years younger I would accept it, and promptly. I would go. I would let somebody else do the oration, but, as for me, I would talk—just talk. I would renew my youth; and talk—and talk—and talk—and have the time of my life! I would march the unforgotten and unforgettable antiques by, and name their names, and give them reverent Hailand-farewell as they passed: Goodman, McCarthy, Gillis, Curry, Baldwin, Winters, Howard, Nye, Stewart; Neely Johnson, Hal Clayton, North, Root,—and my brother, upon whom be peace!—and then the desperadoes, who made life a joy and the "Slaughter-house" a precious possession: Sam Brown, Farmer Pete, Bill Mayfield, Six-fingered Jake, Jack Williams and the rest of the crimson discipleship—and so on and so on. Believe me, I would start a resurrection it would do you more good to look at than the next one will, if you go on the way you are doing now.

Those were the days! those old ones. They will come no more. Youth will come no more. They were so full to the brim with the wine of life; there have been no others like them. It chokes me up to think of them. Would you like me to come out there and cry? It would not beseem my white head.

Good-bye. I drink to you all. Have a good time—and take an old man's blessing.

MARK TWAIN.

A few days later he was writing to H. H. Bancroft, of San Francisco, who had invited him for a visit in event of his coming to the Coast. Henry James had just been there for a week and it was hoped that Howells would soon follow.

To H. H. Bancroft, in San Francisco:

UP IN NEW HAMPSHIRE,

May 27, 1905.

DEAR MR. BANCROFT,—I thank you sincerely for the tempting hospitalities which you offer me, but I have to deny myself, for my wandering days are over, and it is my desire and purpose to sit by the fire the rest of my remnant of life and indulge myself with the pleasure and repose of work—work uninterrupted and unmarred by duties or excursions.

A man who like me, is going to strike 70 on the 30th of next November has no business to be flitting around the way Howells does—that shameless old fictitious butter fly. (But if he comes, don't tell him I said it, for it would hurt him and I wouldn't brush a flake of powder from his wing for anything. I only say it in envy of his indestructible youth, anyway. Howells will be 88 in October.) With thanks again,

Sincerely yours,

S. L. C.

Clemens found that the air of the New Hampshire hills agreed with him and stimulated him to work. He began an entirely new version of

The Mysterious Stranger, of which he already had a bulky and nearly finished manuscript, written in Vienna. He wrote several hundred pages of an extravaganza entitled, Three Thousand Years Among the Microbes, and then, having got his superabundant vitality reduced (it was likely to expend itself in these weird mental exploits), he settled down one day and wrote that really tender and beautiful idyl, Eve's Diary, which he had begun, or at least planned, the previous summer at Tyringham. In a letter to Mr. Frederick A. Duneka, general manager of Harper & Brothers, he tells something of the manner of the story; also his revised opinion of Adam's Diary, written in '93, and originally published as a souvenir of Niagara Falls.

To Frederick A. Duneka, in New York:

DUBLIN, July 16, '05.

DEAR MR. DUNEKA,—I wrote Eve's Diary, she using Adam's Diary as her (unwitting and unconscious) text, of course, since to use any other text would have been an imbecility—then I took Adam's Diary and read it. It turned my stomach. It was not literature; yet it had been literature once—before I sold it to be degraded to an advertisement of the Buffalo Fair. I was going to write and ask you to melt the plates and put it out of print.

But this morning I examined it without temper, and saw that if I abolished the advertisement it would be literature again.

So I have done it. I have struck out 700 words and inserted 5 MS pages of new matter (650 words), and now Adam's Diary is dam good—sixty times as good as it ever was before.

I believe it is as good as Eve's Diary now—no, it's not quite that good, I guess, but it is good enough to go in the same cover with Eve's. I'm sure of that.

I hate to have the old Adam go out any more—don't put it on the presses again, let's put the new one in place of it; and next Xmas, let us bind Adam and Eve in one cover. They score points against each other—so, if not bound together, some of the points would not be perceived.....

P. S. Please send another Adam's Diary, so that I can make 2 revised copies. Eve's Diary is Eve's love-Story, but we will not name it that.

Yrs ever,

MARK.

The peace-making at Portsmouth between Japan and Russia was not satisfactory to Mark Twain, who had fondly hoped there would be no peace until, as he said, "Russian liberty was safe. One more battle would have abolished the waiting chains of millions upon millions of unborn Russians and I wish it could have been fought." He set down an expression of his feelings for the Associated Press, and it invited many letters. Charles Francis Adams wrote, "It attracted my attention because it so exactly expresses the views I have myself all along entertained."

Clemens was invited by Colonel George Harvey to dine with the Russian emissaries, Baron Rosen and Sergius Witte. He declined, but his telegram so pleased Witte that he asked permission to publish it, and announced that he would show it to the Czar.

Telegram. To Col. George Harvey, in New York:

TO COLONEL HARVEY,—I am still a cripple, otherwise I should be more than glad of this opportunity to meet the illustrious magicians who came here equipped with nothing but a pen, and with it have divided the honors of the war with the sword. It is fair to presume that in thirty centuries history will not get done admiring these men who attempted what the world regarded as impossible and achieved it.

Witte would not have cared to show the Czar the telegram in its original form, which follows.

Telegram (unsent). To Col. George Harvey, in New York:

TO COLONEL HARVEY,—I am still a cripple, otherwise I should be more than glad of this opportunity to meet those illustrious magicians who with the pen have annulled, obliterated, and abolished every high achievement of the Japanese sword and turned the tragedy of a tremendous war into a gay and blithesome comedy. If I may, let me in all respect and honor salute them as my fellow-humorists, I taking third place, as becomes one who was not born to modesty, but by diligence and hard work is acquiring it. MARK.

Nor still another unsent form, perhaps more characteristic than either of the foregoing.

Telegram (unsent). To Col. George Harvey, in New York:

DEAR COLONEL,—No, this is a love-feast; when you call a lodge of sorrow send for me.

MARK.

To Mrs. Crane, Quarry Farm:

DUBLIN, Sept. 24, '05.

Susy dear, I have had a lovely dream. Livy, dressed in black, was sitting up in my bed (here) at my right and looking as young and sweet as she used to do when she was in health. She said: "what is the name of your sweet sister?" I said, "Pamela." "Oh, yes, that is it, I thought it was—" (naming a name which has escaped me) "Won't you write it down for me?" I reached eagerly for a pen and pad—laid my hands upon both—then said to myself, "It is only a dream," and turned back sorrowfully and there she was, still. The conviction flamed through me that our lamented disaster was a dream, and this a reality. I said, "How blessed it is, how blessed it is, it was all a dream, only a dream!" She only smiled and did not ask what dream I meant, which surprised me. She leaned her head against mine and I kept saying, "I was perfectly sure it was a dream, I never would have believed it wasn't."

I think she said several things, but if so they are gone from my memory. I woke and did not know I had been dreaming. She was gone. I wondered how she could go without my knowing it, but I did not spend any thought upon that, I was too busy thinking of how vivid and real was the dream that we had lost her and how unspeakably blessed it was to find that it was not true and that she was still ours and with us.

S. L. C.

One day that summer Mark Twain received a letter from the actress, Minnie Maddern Fiske, asking him to write something that would aid her in her crusade against bull-fighting. The idea appealed to him; he replied at once.

To Mrs. Fiske:

DEAR MRS. FISKE,—I shall certainly write the story. But I may not get it to suit me, in which case it will go in the fire. Later I will try again—and yet again—and again. I am used to this. It has taken me twelve years to write a short story—the shortest one I ever wrote, I think.—[Probably "The Death Disk."]—So do not be discouraged; I will stick to this one in the same way. Sincerely yours,

S. L. CLEMENS.

He did not delay in his beginning, and a few weeks later was sending word to his publisher about it.

To Frederick A. Duneka, in New York:

Oct. 2, '05.

DEAR MR. DUNEKA,—I have just finished a short story which I "greatly admire," and so will you—"A Horse's Tale"—about 15,000 words, at a rough guess. It has good fun in it, and several characters, and is lively. I shall finish revising it in a few days or more, then Jean will type it.

Don't you think you can get it into the Jan. and Feb. numbers and issue it as a dollar booklet just after the middle of Jan. when you issue the Feb. number?

It ought to be ably illustrated.

Why not sell simultaneous rights, for this once, to the Ladies' Home Journal or Collier's, or both, and recoup yourself?—for I would like to get it to classes that can't afford Harper's. Although it doesn't preach, there's a sermon concealed in it.

Yr sincerely,

MARK.

Five days later he added some rather interesting facts concerning the new story.

To F. A. Duneka, in New York:

Oct. 7, 1906. ['05]

DEAR MR. DUNEKA,—... I've made a poor guess as to number of words. I think there must be 20,000. My usual page of MS. contains about 130 words; but when I am deeply interested in my work and dead to everything else, my hand-writing shrinks and shrinks until there's a great deal more than 130 on a page—oh, yes, a deal more. Well, I discover, this morning, that this tale is written in that small hand.

This strong interest is natural, for the heroine is my daughter, Susy, whom we lost. It was not intentional—it was a good while before I found it out.

So I am sending you her picture to use—and to reproduce with photographic exactness the unsurpassable expression and all. May you find an artist who has lost an idol!

Take as good care of the picture as you can and restore it to me when I come.

I hope you will illustrate this tale considerably. Not humorous pictures. No. When they are good (or bad) one's humor gets no chance to play surprises on the reader. A humorous subject illustrated seriously is all right, but a humorous artist is no fit person for such work. You see, the humorous writer pretends to absolute seriousness (when he knows his trade) then for an artist—to step in and give his calculated gravity all away with a funny picture—oh, my land! It gives me the dry gripes just to think of it. It would be just about up to the average comic artist's intellectual level to make a funny picture of the horse kicking the lungs out of a trader. Hang it, the remark is funny—because the horse is not aware of it but the fact is not humorous, it is tragic and it is no subject for a humorous picture.

Could I be allowed to sit in judgment upon the pictures before they are accepted—at least those in which Cathy may figure?

This is not essential. It is but a suggestion, and it is hereby withdrawn, if it would be troublesome or cause delay.

I hope you will reproduce the cat-pile, full page. And save the photo for me in as good condition as possible. When Susy and Clara were little tots those cats had their profoundest worship, and there is no duplicate of this picture. These cats all had thundering names, or inappropriate ones—

furnished by the children with my help. One was named Buffalo Bill.

Are you interested in coincidences?

After discovering, about the middle of the book, that Cathy was Susy Clemens, I put her picture with my MS., to be reproduced. After the book was finished it was discovered that Susy had a dim model of Soldier Boy in her arms; I had forgotten all about that toy.

Then I examined the cat-picture and laid it with the MS. for introduction; but it was not until yesterday that I remembered that one of the cats was named Buffalo Bill.

Sincerely yours,

MARK.

The reference in this letter to shrinkage of his hand-writing with the increasing intensity of his interest, and the consequent addition of the number of words to the page, recalls another fact, noted by Mr. Duneka, viz.: that because of his terse Anglo-Saxon diction, Mark Twain could put more words on a magazine page than any other writer. It is hardly necessary to add that he got more force into what he put on the page for the same reason.

There was always a run of reporters at Mark Twain's New York home. His opinion was sought for on every matter of public interest, and whatever happened to him in particular was considered good for at least half a column of copy, with his name as a catch-line at the top. When it was learned that he was to spend the summer in New Hampshire, the reporters had all wanted to find out about it. Now that the summer was ending, they began to want to know how he had liked it, what work he had done and what were his plans for another year. As they frequently applied to his publishers for these details it was finally suggested to him that he write a letter furnishing the required information. His reply, handed to Mr. Duneka, who was visiting him at the moment, is full of interest.

Mem. for Mr. Duneka:

DUBLIN, Oct. 9, 1905.

... As to the other matters, here are the details.

Yes, I have tried a number of summer homes, here and in Europe together.

Each of these homes had charms of its own; charms and delights of its own, and some of them—even in Europe had comforts. Several of them had conveniences, too. They all had a "view."

It is my conviction that there should always be some water in a view—a lake or a river, but not the ocean, if you are down on its level. I think that when you are down on its level it seldom inflames you with an ecstasy which you could not get out of a sand-flat. It is like being on board ship, over again; indeed it is worse than that, for there's three months of it. On board ship one tires of the aspects in a couple of days, and quits looking. The same vast circle of heaving humps is spread around you all the time, with you in the centre of it and never gaining an inch on the horizon, so far as you can see; for variety, a flight of flying-fish, mornings; a flock of porpoises throwing summersaults afternoons; a remote whale spouting, Sundays; occasional phosphorescent effects, nights; every other day a streak of black smoke trailing along under the horizon; on the one single red letter day, the illustrious iceberg. I have seen that iceberg thirty-four times in thirty-seven voyages; it is always the same shape, it is always the same size, it always throws up the same old flash when the sun strikes it; you may set it on any New York door-step of a June morning and light it up with a mirror-flash; and I will engage to recognize it. It is artificial, and it is provided and anchored out by the steamer companies. I used to like the sea, but I was young then, and could easily get excited over any kind of monotony, and keep it up till the monotonies ran out, if it was a fortnight.

Last January, when we were beginning to inquire about a home for this summer, I remembered that Abbott Thayer had said, three years before, that the New Hampshire highlands was a good place. He was right—it was a good place. Any place that is good for an artist in paint is good for an artist in morals and ink. Brush is here, too; so is Col. T. W. Higginson; so is Raphael Pumpelly; so is Mr. Secretary Hitchcock; so is Henderson; so is Learned; so is Summer; so is Franklin MacVeigh; so is Joseph L. Smith; so is Henry Copley Greene, when I am not occupying his house, which I am doing this season. Paint, literature, science, statesmanship, history, professorship, law, morals,—these are all represented here, yet crime is substantially unknown.

The summer homes of these refugees are sprinkled, a mile apart, among the forest-clad hills, with access to each other by firm smooth country roads which are so embowered in dense foliage that it is always twilight in there, and comfortable. The forests are spider-webbed with these good roads, they go everywhere; but for the help of the guide-boards, the stranger would not arrive anywhere.

The village—Dublin—is bunched together in its own place, but a good telephone service makes its markets handy to all those outliars. I have spelt it that way to be witty. The village executes orders on, the Boston plan—promptness and courtesy.

The summer homes are high-perched, as a rule, and have contenting outlooks. The house we occupy has one. Monadnock, a soaring double hump, rises into the sky at its left elbow—that is to say, it is close at hand. From the base of the long slant of the mountain the valley spreads away to the circling frame of the hills, and beyond the frame the billowy sweep of remote great ranges rises to view and flows, fold upon fold, wave upon wave, soft and blue and unwordly, to the horizon fifty miles away. In these October days

Monadnock and the valley and its framing hills make an inspiring picture to look at, for they are sumptuously splashed and mottled and be-torched from sky-line to sky-line with the richest dyes the autumn can furnish; and when they lie flaming in the full drench of the mid-afternoon sun, the sight affects the spectator physically, it stirs his blood like military music.

These summer homes are commodious, well built, and well furnished—facts which sufficiently indicate that the owners built them to live in themselves. They have furnaces and wood fireplaces, and the rest of the comforts and conveniences of a city home, and can be comfortably occupied all the year round.

We cannot have this house next season, but I have secured Mrs. Upton's house which is over in the law and science quarter, two or three miles from here, and about the same distance from the art, literary, and scholastic groups. The science and law quarter has needed improving, this good while.

The nearest railway-station is distant something like an hour's drive; it is three hours from there to Boston, over a branch line. You can go to New York in six hours per branch lines if you change cars every time you think of it, but it is better to go to Boston and stop over and take the trunk line next day, then you do not get lost.

It is claimed that the atmosphere of the New Hampshire highlands is exceptionally bracing and stimulating, and a fine aid to hard and continuous work. It is a just claim, I think. I came in May, and wrought 35 successive days without a break. It is possible that I could not have done it elsewhere. I do not know; I have not had any disposition to try it, before. I think I got the disposition out of the atmosphere, this time. I feel quite sure, in fact, that that is where it came from.

I am ashamed to confess what an intolerable pile of manuscript I ground out in the 35 days, therefore I will keep the number of words to myself. I wrote the first half of a long tale—"The Adventures of a Microbe" and put it away for a finish next summer, and started another long tale—"The Mysterious Stranger;" I wrote the first half of it and put it with the other for a finish next summer. I stopped, then. I was not tired, but I had no books on hand that needed finishing this year except one that was seven years old. After a little I took that one up and finished it. Not for publication, but to have it ready for revision next summer.

Since I stopped work I have had a two months' holiday. The summer has been my working time for 35 years; to have a holiday in it (in America) is new for me. I have not broken it, except to write "Eve's Diary" and "A Horse's Tale"—short things occupying the mill 12 days.

This year our summer is 6 months long and ends with November and the flight home to New York, but next year we hope and expect to stretch it another month and end it the first of December.

[No signature.]

The fact that he was a persistent smoker was widely known, and many friends and admirers of Mark Twain sent him cigars, most of which he could not use, because they were too good. He did not care for Havana cigars, but smoked the fragrant, inexpensive domestic tobacco with plenty of "pep" in it, as we say today. Now and then he had an opportunity to head off some liberal friend, who wrote asking permission to contribute to his cigar collection, as instance the following.

To Rev. L. M. Powers, in Haverhill, Mass.:

Nov. 9, 1905.

DEAR MR. POWERS,—I should accept your hospitable offer at once but for the fact I couldn't do it and remain honest. That is to say if I allowed you to send me what you believe to be good cigars it would distinctly mean that I meant to smoke them, whereas I should do nothing of the kind. I know a good cigar better than you do, for I have had 60 years experience.

No, that is not what I mean; I mean I know a bad cigar better than anybody else; I judge by the price only; if it costs above 5 cents I know it to be either foreign or half-foreign, and unsmokeable. By me I have many boxes of Havana cigars, of all prices from 20 cts apiece up to 1.66 apiece; I bought none of them, they were all presents, they are an accumulation of several years. I have never smoked one of them and never shall, I work them off on the visitor. You shall have a chance when you come.

Pessimists are born not made; optimists are born not made; but no man is born either pessimist wholly or optimist wholly, perhaps; he is pessimistic along certain lines and optimistic along certain others. That is my case.

Sincerely yours,

S. L. CLEMENS.

In spite of all the fine photographs that were made of him, there recurred constantly among those sent him to be autographed a print of one which, years before, Sarony had made and placed on public sale. It was a good photograph, mechanically and even artistically, but it did not please Mark Twain. Whenever he saw it he recalled Sarony with bitterness and severity. Once he received an inquiry concerning it, and thus feelingly expressed himself.

To Mr. Row (no address):

21 FIFTH AVENUE, NEW YORK,

November 14, 1905.

DEAR MR. ROW,—That alleged portrait has a private history. Sarony was as much of an enthusiast about wild animals as he was about photography; and when Du Chaillu brought the first Gorilla to this country in 1819 he came to me in a fever of excitement and asked me if my father was of record and authentic. I said he was; then Sarony, without any abatement of his excitement asked if my grandfather also was of record and authentic. I said he was. Then Sarony, with still rising excitement and with joy added to it, said he had found my great grandfather in the person of the gorilla, and had recognized him at once by his resemblance to me. I was deeply hurt but did not reveal this, because I knew Saxony meant no offense for the gorilla had not done him any harm, and he was not a man who would say an unkind thing about a gorilla wantonly. I went with him to inspect the ancestor, and examined him from several points of view, without being able to detect anything more than a passing resemblance. "Wait," said Sarony with confidence, "let me show you." He borrowed my overcoat—and put it on the gorilla. The result was surprising. I saw that the gorilla while not looking distinctly like me was exactly what my great grand father would have looked like if I had had one. Sarong photographed the creature in that overcoat, and spread the picture about the world. It has remained spread about the world ever since. It turns up every week in some newspaper somewhere or other. It is not my favorite, but to my exasperation it is everybody else's. Do you think you could get it suppressed for me? I will pay the limit.

Sincerely yours,

S. L. CLEMENS.

The year 1905 closed triumphantly for Mark Twain. The great "Seventieth Birthday" dinner planned by Colonel George Harvey is remembered to-day as the most notable festival occasion in New York literary history. Other dinners and ovations followed. At seventy he had returned to the world, more beloved, more honored than ever before.

XLV. LETTERS, 1906, TO VARIOUS PERSONS. THE FAREWELL LECTURE. A SECOND SUMMER IN DUBLIN. BILLIARDS AND COPYRIGHT.

MARK TWAIN at "Pier Seventy," as he called it, paused to look backward and to record some memoirs of his long, eventful past. The Autobiography dictations begun in Florence were resumed, and daily he traveled back, recalling long-ago scenes and all-but-forgotten places. He was not without reminders. Now and again there came some message that brought back the old days—the Tom Sawyer and Huck Finn days—or the romance of the river that he never recalled other than with tenderness and a tone of regret that it was gone. An invitation to the golden wedding of two ancient friends moved and saddened him, and his answer to it conveys about all the story of life.

To Mr. and Mrs. Gordon:

21 FIFTH AVENUE,

Jan. 24, '06.

DEAR GORDONS,—I have just received your golden-wedding "At Home" and am trying to adjust my focus to it and realize how much it means. It is inconceivable! With a simple sweep it carries me back over a stretch of time measurable only in astronomical terms and geological periods. It brings before me Mrs. Gordon, young, round-limbed, handsome; and with her the Youngbloods and their two babies, and Laura Wright, that unspoiled little maid, that fresh flower of the woods and the prairies. Forty-eight years ago!

Life was a fairy-tale, then, it is a tragedy now. When I was 43 and John Hay 41 he said life was a tragedy after 40, and I disputed it. Three years ago he asked me to testify again: I counted my graves, and there was nothing for me to say.

I am old; I recognize it but I don't realize it. I wonder if a person ever really ceases to feel young—I mean, for a whole day at a time. My love to you both, and to all of us that are left.

MARK.

Though he used very little liquor of any kind, it was Mark Twain's custom to keep a bottle of Scotch whiskey with his collection of pipes and cigars and tobacco on a little table by his bed-side. During restless nights he found a small quantity of it conducive to sleep. Andrew Carnegie, learning of this custom, made it his business to supply Scotch of his own special importation. The first case came, direct from Scotland. When it arrived Clemens sent this characteristic acknowledgment.

To Andrew Carnegie, in Scotland:

21 FIFTH AVE. Feb. 10, '06.

DEAR ST. ANDREW,—The whisky arrived in due course from over the water; last week one bottle of it was extracted from the wood and inserted into me, on the instalment plan, with this result: that I believe it to be the best, smoothest whisky now on the planet. Thanks, oh, thanks: I have discarded Peruna.

Hoping that you three are well and happy and will be coming back before the winter sets in.

I am,

Sincerely yours,

MARK.

It must have been a small bottle to be consumed by him in a week, or perhaps he had able assistance. The next brief line refers to the manuscript of his article, "Saint Joan of Arc," presented to the museum at Rouen.

To Edward E. Clarke:

21 FIFTH AVE., Feb., 1906.

DEAR SIR,—I have found the original manuscript and with great pleasure I transmit it herewith, also a printed copy.

It is a matter of great pride to me to have any word of mine concerning the world's supremest heroine honored by a place in that Museum.

Sincerely yours,

S. L. CLEMENS.

The series of letters which follows was prepared by Mark Twain and General Fred Grant, mainly with a view of advertising the lecture that Clemens had agreed to deliver for the benefit of the Robert Fulton Monument Association. It was, in fact, to be Mark Twain's "farewell lecture," and the association had really proposed to pay him a thousand dollars for it. The exchange of these letters, however, was never made outside of Mark Twain's bed-room. Propped against the pillows, pen in hand, with General Grant beside him, they arranged the series with the idea of publication. Later the plan was discarded, so that this pleasant foolery appears here for the first, time.

PRIVATE AND CONFIDENTIAL

(Correspondence)

Telegram

Army Headquarters (date)

MARK TWAIN, New York,—Would you consider a proposal to talk at Carnegie Hall for the benefit of the Robert Fulton Monument Association, of which you are a Vice President, for a fee of a thousand dollars?

F. D. GRANT,

President,

Fulton Monument Association.

Telegraphic Answer:

MAJOR-GENERAL F. D. GRANT, Army Headquarters,—I shall be glad to do it, but I must stipulate that you keep the thousand dollars and add it to the Monument fund as my contribution.

CLEMENS.

Letters:

DEAR MR. CLEMENS,—You have the thanks of the Association, and the terms shall be as you say. But why give all of it? Why not reserve a portion—why should you do this work wholly without compensation?

Truly yours

FRED. D. GRANT.

MAJOR GENERAL GRANT, Army Headquarters.

DEAR GENERAL,—Because I stopped talking for pay a good many years ago, and I could not resume the habit now without a great deal of personal discomfort. I love to hear myself talk, because I get so much instruction and moral upheaval out of it, but I lose the bulk of this joy when I charge for it. Let the terms stand.

General, if I have your approval, I wish to use this good occasion to retire permanently from the platform.

Truly yours

S. L. CLEMENS.

DEAR MR. CLEMENS,—Certainly. But as an old friend, permit me to say, Don't do that. Why should you?—you are not old yet.

Yours truly,

FRED D. GRANT.

DEAR GENERAL,—I mean the pay-platform; I shan't retire from the gratis-platform until after I am dead and courtesy requires me to keep still and not disturb the others.

What shall I talk about? My idea is this: to instruct the audience about Robert Fulton, and.... Tell me—was that his real name, or was it his nom de plume? However, never mind, it is not important—I can skip it, and the house will think I knew all about it, but forgot. Could you find out for me if he was one of the Signers of the Declaration, and which one? But if it is any trouble, let it alone, I can skip it. Was he out with Paul Jones? Will you ask Horace Porter? And ask him if he brought both of them home. These will be very interesting facts, if they can be established. But never mind, don't trouble Porter, I can establish them anyway. The way I look at it, they are historical gems—gems of the very first water.

Well, that is my idea, as I have said: first, excite the audience with a spoonful of information about Fulton, then quiet down with a barrel of illustration drawn by memory from my books—and if you don't say anything the house will think they never heard of it before, because people don't really read your books, they only say they do, to keep you from feeling bad. Next, excite the house with another spoonful of Fultonian fact, then tranquilize them again with another barrel of illustration. And so on and so on, all through the evening; and if you are discreet and don't tell them the illustrations don't illustrate anything, they won't notice it and I will send them home as well-informed about Robert Fulton as I am myself. Don't be afraid; I know all about audiences, they believe everything you say, except when you are telling the truth.

Truly yours,

S. L. CLEMENS.

P.S. Mark all the advertisements "Private and Confidential," otherwise the people will not read them.

M. T.

DEAR MR. CLEMENS,—How long shall you talk? I ask in order that we may be able to say when carriages may be called.

Very Truly yours,

HUGH GORDON MILLER,

Secretary.

DEAR MR. MILLER,—I cannot say for sure. It is my custom to keep on talking till I get the audience cowed. Sometimes it takes an hour and fifteen minutes, sometimes I can do it in an hour.

Sincerely yours,

S. L. CLEMENS.

Mem. My charge is 2 boxes free. Not the choicest—sell the choicest, and give me any 6-seat boxes you please.

S. L. C.

I want Fred Grant (in uniform) on the stage; also the rest of the officials of the Association; also other distinguished people—all the attractions we can get. Also, a seat for Mr. Albert Bigelow Paine, who may be useful to me if he is near me and on the front.

S. L. C.

The seat chosen for the writer of these notes was to be at the front of the stage in order that the lecturer might lean over now and then and pretend to be asking information concerning Fulton. I was not entirely happy in the thought of this showy honor, and breathed more freely when this plan was abandoned and the part assigned to General Grant.

The lecture was given in Carnegie Hall, which had been gayly decorated for the occasion. The house was more than filled, and a great sum of money was realized for the fund.

It was that spring that Gorky and Tchaikowski, the Russian revolutionists, came to America hoping to arouse interest in their cause. The idea of the overthrow of the Russian dynasty was pleasant to Mark Twain. Few things would have given him greater comfort than to have known that a little more than ten years would see the downfall of Russian imperialism. The letter which follows was a reply to an invitation from Tchaikowski, urging him to speak at one of the meetings.

DEAR MR. TCHAIKOWSKI,—I thank you for the honor of the invitation, but I am not able to accept it, because on Thursday evening I shall be presiding at a meeting whose object is to find remunerative work for certain classes of our blind who would gladly support themselves if they had the opportunity.

My sympathies are with the Russian revolution, of course. It goes without saying. I hope it will succeed, and now that I have talked with you I take heart to believe it will. Government by falsified promises; by lies, by treacheries, and by the butcher-knife for the aggrandizement of a single family of drones and its idle and vicious kin has been borne quite long enough in Russia, I should think, and it is to be hoped that the roused nation, now rising in its strength, will presently put an end to it and set up the republic in its place. Some of us, even of the white headed, may live to see the blessed day when Czars and Grand Dukes will be as scarce there as I trust they are in heaven.

Most sincerely yours,

MARK TWAIN.

There came another summer at Dublin, New Hampshire, this time in the fine Upton residence on the other slope of Monadnock, a place of equally beautiful surroundings, and an even more extended view. Clemens was at this time working steadily on his so-called Autobiography, which was not that, in fact, but a series of remarkable chapters, reminiscent, reflective, commentative, written without any particular sequence as to time or subject-matter. He dictated these chapters to a stenographer, usually in the open air, sitting in a comfortable rocker or pacing up and down the long veranda that faced a vast expanse of wooded slope and lake and distant blue mountains. It became one of the happiest occupations of his later years.

To W. D. Howells, in Maine:

DUBLIN, Sunday, June 17, '06.

DEAR HOWELLS,—..... The dictating goes lazily and pleasantly on. With intervals. I find that I have been at it, off and on, nearly two hours a day for 155 days, since Jan. 9. To be exact I've dictated 75 hours in 80 days and loafed 75 days. I've added 60,000 words in the month that I've been here; which indicates that I've dictated during 20 days of that time—40 hours, at an average of 1,500 words an hour. It's a plenty, and I am satisfied.

There's a good deal of "fat" I've dictated, (from Jan. 9) 210,000 words, and the "fat" adds about 50,000 more.

The "fat" is old pigeon-holed things, of the years gone by, which I or editors didn't das't to print. For instance, I am dumping in the little old book which I read to you in Hartford about 30 years ago and which you said "publish—and ask Dean Stanley to furnish an introduction; he'll do it." ("Captain Stormfield's Visit to Heaven.") It reads quite to suit me, without altering a word, now that it isn't to see print until I am dead.

To-morrow I mean to dictate a chapter which will get my heirs and assigns burnt alive if they venture to print it this side of 2006 A.D.—which I judge they won't. There'll be lots of such chapters if I live 3 or 4 years longer. The edition of A.D. 2006 will make a stir when it comes out. I shall be hovering around taking notice, along with other dead pals. You are invited.

MARK.

His tendency to estimate the measure of the work he was doing, and had completed, must have clung to him from his old printer days.

The chapter which was to get his heirs and assigns burned alive was on the orthodox God, and there was more than one such chapter. In the next letter he refers to two exquisite poems by Howells, and the writer of these notes recalls his wonderful reading of them aloud. 'In Our Town' was a collection of short stories then recently issued by William Allen White. Howells had recommended them.

To W. D. Howells, in Maine:

21 FIFTH AVE., Tuesday Eve.

DEAR HOWELLS,—It is lovely of you to say those beautiful things—I don't know how to thank you enough. But I love you, that I know.

I read "After the Wedding" aloud and we felt all the pain of it and the truth. It was very moving and very beautiful—would have been over-comingly moving, at times, but for the haltings and pauses compelled by the difficulties of MS—these were a protection, in that they furnished me time to brace up my voice, and get a new start. Jean wanted to keep the MS for another reading-aloud, and for "keeps," too, I suspected, but I said it would be safest to write you about it.

I like "In Our Town," particularly that Colonel, of the Lookout Mountain Oration, and very particularly pages 212-16. I wrote and told White so.

After "After the Wedding" I read "The Mother" aloud and sounded its human deeps with your deep-sea lead. I had not read it before, since it was first published.

I have been dictating some fearful things, for 4 successive mornings—for no eye but yours to see until I have been dead a century—if then. But I got them out of my system, where they had been festering for years—and that was the main thing. I feel better, now.

I came down today on business—from house to house in 12 1/2 hours, and expected to arrive dead, but am neither tired nor sleepy.

Yours as always

MARK.

To William Allen White, in Emporia, Kans.:

DUBLIN, NEW HAMPSHIRE,

June 24, 1906.

DEAR MR. WHITE,—Howells told me that "In Our Town" was a charming book, and indeed it is. All of it is delightful when read one's self, parts of it can score finely when subjected to the most exacting of tests—the reading aloud. Pages 197 and 216 are of that grade. I have tried them a couple of times on the family, and pages 212 and 216 are qualified to fetch any house of any country, caste or color, endowed with those riches which are denied to no nation on the planet—humor and feeling.

Talk again—the country is listening.

Sincerely yours,

S. L. CLEMENS.

Witter Bynner, the poet, was one of the editors of McClure's Magazine at this time, but was trying to muster the courage to give up routine work for verse-making and the possibility of poverty. Clemens was fond of Bynner and believed in his work. He did not advise him, however, to break away entirely from a salaried position—at least not immediately; but one day Bynner did so, and reported the step he had taken, with some doubt as to the answer he would receive.

To Witter Bynner, in New York:

DUBLIN, Oct. 5, 1906.

DEAR POET,—You have certainly done right for several good reasons; at least, of them, I can name two:

1. With your reputation you can have your freedom and yet earn your living. 2. if you fall short of succeeding to your wish, your reputation will provide you another job. And so in high approval I suppress the scolding and give you the saintly and fatherly pat instead.

MARK TWAIN.

On another occasion, when Bynner had written a poem to Clara Clemens, her father pretended great indignation that the first poem written by Bynner to any one in his household should not be to him, and threatened revenge. At dinner shortly after he produced from his pocket a slip of paper on which he had set down what he said was "his only poem." He read the lines that follow:

"Of all sad words of tongue or pen,
The saddest are these: It might have been.
Ah, say not so! as life grows longer, leaner, thinner,
We recognize, O God, it might have Bynner!"

He returned to New York in October and soon after was presented by Mrs. H. H. Rogers with a handsome billiard-table.

He had a passion for the game, but had played comparatively little since the old Hartford days of fifteen years before, when a group of his friends used to assemble on Friday nights in the room at the top of the house for long, strenuous games and much hilarity. Now the old fever all came back; the fascinations of the game superseded even his interest in the daily dictations.

To Mrs. H. H. Rogers, in New York:

21 FIFTH AVENUE, Monday, Nov., 1906.

DEAR MRS. ROGERS,—The billiard table is better than the doctors. It is driving out the heartburn in a most promising way. I have a billiardist on the premises, and I walk not less than ten miles every day with the cue in my hand. And the walking is not the whole of the exercise, nor the most health-giving part of it, I think. Through the multitude of the positions and attitudes it brings into play every muscle in the body and exercises them all.

The games begin right after luncheon, daily, and continue until midnight, with 2 hours' intermission for dinner and music. And so it is 9 hours' exercise per day, and 10 or 12 on Sunday. Yesterday and last night it was 12—and I slept until 8 this morning without waking. The billiard table, as a Sabbath breaker can beat any coal-breaker in Pennsylvania, and give it 30 in, the game. If Mr. Rogers will take to daily billiards he can do without doctors and the massageur, I think.

We are really going to build a house on my farm, an hour and a half from New York. It is decided. It is to be built by contract, and is to come within $25,000.

With love and many thanks.

S. L. C.

P.S. Clara is in the sanitarium—till January 28 when her western concert tour will begin. She is getting to be a mighty competent singer. You must know Clara better; she is one of the very finest and completest and most satisfactory characters I have ever met. Others knew it before, but I have always been busy with other matters.

The "billiardist on the premises" was the writer of these notes, who, earlier in the year, had become his biographer, and, in the course of time, his daily companion and friend. The farm mentioned was one which he had bought at Redding, Connecticut, where, later, he built the house known as "Stormfield."

Henry Mills Alden, for nearly forty years editor of Harper's

Magazine, arrived at his seventieth birthday on November 11th that year, and Harper & Brothers had arranged to give him a great dinner in the offices of Franklin Square, where, for half a century, he had been an active force. Mark Twain, threatened with a cold, and knowing the dinner would be strenuous, did not feel able to attend, so wrote a letter which, if found suitable, could be read at the gathering.

To Mr. Henry Alden:

ALDEN,—dear and ancient friend—it is a solemn moment. You have now reached the age of discretion. You have been a long time arriving. Many years ago you docked me on an article because the subject was too old; later, you docked me on an article because the subject was too new; later still, you docked me on an article because the subject was betwixt and between. Once, when I wrote a Letter to Queen Victoria, you did not put it in the respectable part of the Magazine, but interred it in that potter's field, the Editor's Drawer. As a result, she never answered it. How often we recall, with regret, that Napoleon once shot at a magazine editor and missed him and killed a publisher. But we remember, with charity, that his intentions were good.

You will reform, now, Alden. You will cease from these economies, and you will be discharged. But in your retirement you will carry with you the admiration and earnest good wishes of the oppressed and toiling scribes. This will be better than bread. Let this console you when the bread fails.

You will carry with you another thing, too—the affection of the scribes; for they all love you in spite of your crimes. For you bear a kind heart in your breast, and the sweet and winning spirit that charms away all hostilities and animosities, and makes of your enemy your friend and keeps him so. You have reigned over us thirty-six years, and, please God, you shall reign another thirty-six—"and peace to Mahmoud on his golden throne!"

Always yours

MARK

A copyright bill was coming up in Washington and a delegation of authors went down to work for it. Clemens was not the head of the delegation, but he was the most prominent member of it, as well as the most useful. He invited the writer to accompany him, and elsewhere I have told in detail the story of that excursion,—[See Mark Twain; A Biography, chap. ccli,]—which need be but briefly touched upon here.

His work was mainly done aside from that of the delegation. They had him scheduled for a speech, however, which he made without notes and with scarcely any preparation. Meantime he had applied to Speaker Cannon for permission to allow him on the floor of the House, where he could buttonhole the Congressmen. He was not eligible to the floor without having received the thanks of Congress, hence the following letter:

To Hon. Joseph Cannon, House of Representatives:

Dec. 7, 1906.

DEAR UNCLE JOSEPH,—Please get me the thanks of the Congress—not next week but right away. It is very necessary. Do accomplish this for your affectionate old friend right away; by persuasion, if you can, by violence if you must, for it is imperatively necessary that I get on the floor for two or three hours and talk to the members, man by man, in behalf of the support, encouragement and protection of one of the nation's most valuable assets and industries—its literature. I have arguments with me, also a barrel, with liquid in it.

Give me a chance. Get me the thanks of Congress. Don't wait for others; there isn't time. I have stayed away and let Congress alone for seventy-one years and I am entitled to thanks. Congress knows it perfectly well and I have long felt hurt that this quite proper and earned expression of gratitude has been merely felt by the House and never publicly uttered. Send me an order on the Sergeant-at-Arms quick. When shall I come? With love and a benediction.

MARK TWAIN.

This was mainly a joke. Mark Twain did not expect any "thanks," but he did hope for access to the floor, which once, in an earlier day, had been accorded him. We drove to the Capitol and he delivered his letter to "Uncle Joe" by hand. "Uncle Joe" could not give him the privilege of the floor; the rules had become more stringent. He declared they would hang him if he did such a thing. He added that he had a private room down-stairs, where Mark Twain might establish headquarters, and that he would assign his colored servant, Neal, of long acquaintanceship with many of the members, to pass the word that Mark Twain was receiving.

The result was a great success. All that afternoon members of Congress poured into the Speaker's room and, in an atmosphere blue with tobacco smoke, Mark Twain talked the gospel of copyright to his heart's content.

The bill did not come up for passage that session, but Mark Twain lived to see his afternoon's lobbying bring a return. In 1909, Champ Clark, and those others who had gathered around him that afternoon, passed a measure that added fourteen years to the copyright term.

The next letter refers to a proposed lobby of quite a different sort.

To Helen Keller, in Wrentham, Mass.:

21 FIFTH AVENUE,

Dec. 23, '06.

DEAR HELEN KELLER,—... You say, "As a reformer, you know that ideas must be driven home again and again."

Yes, I know it; and by old experience I know that speeches and documents and public meetings are a pretty poor and lame way of accomplishing it. Last year I proposed a sane way—one which I had practiced with success for a quarter of a century—but I wasn't expecting it to get any attention, and it didn't.

Give me a battalion of 200 winsome young girls and matrons, and let me tell them what to do and how to do it, and I will be responsible for shining results. If I could mass them on the stage in front of the audience and instruct them there, I could make a public meeting take hold of itself and do something really valuable for once. Not that the real instruction would be done there, for it wouldn't; it would be previously done privately, and merely repeated there.

But it isn't going to happen—the good old way will be stuck to: there'll be a public meeting: with music, and prayer, and a wearying report, and a verbal description of the marvels the blind can do, and 17 speeches—then the call upon all present who are still alive, to contribute. This hoary program was invented in the idiot asylum, and will never be changed. Its function is to breed hostility to good causes.

Some day somebody will recruit my 200—my dear beguilesome Knights of the Golden Fleece—and you will see them make good their ominous name.

Mind, we must meet! not in the grim and ghastly air of the platform, mayhap, but by the friendly fire—here at 21.

Affectionately your friend,

S. L. CLEMENS.

They did meet somewhat later that winter in the friendly parlors of No. 21, and friends gathered in to meet the marvelous blind girl and to pay tribute to Miss Sullivan (Mrs. Macy) for her almost incredible achievement.

MARK TWAIN'S LETTERS—1853-1866

VOLUME 6

XLVI. LETTERS 1907-08. A DEGREE FROM OXFORD. THE NEW HOME AT REDDING.

The author, J. Howard Moore, sent a copy of his book, The Universal Kinship, with a letter in which he said: "Most humorists have no anxiety except to glorify themselves and add substance to their pocket-books by making their readers laugh. You have shown, on many occasions, that your mission is not simply to antidote the melancholy of a world, but includes a real and intelligent concern for the general welfare of your fellowman."

The Universal Kinship was the kind of a book that Mark Twain appreciated, as his acknowledgment clearly shows.

To Mr. J. Howard Moore:

Feb. 2, '07.

DEAR MR. MOORE, The book has furnished me several days of deep pleasure and satisfaction; it has compelled my gratitude at the same time, since it saves me the labor of stating my own long-cherished opinions and reflections and resentments by doing it lucidly and fervently and irascibly for me.

There is one thing that always puzzles me: as inheritors of the mentality of our reptile ancestors we have improved the inheritance by a thousand grades; but in the matter of the morals which they left us we have gone backward as many grades. That evolution is strange, and to me unaccountable and unnatural. Necessarily we started equipped with their perfect and blemishless morals; now we are wholly destitute; we have no real, morals, but only artificial ones—morals created and preserved by the forced suppression of natural and hellish instincts. Yet we are dull enough to be vain of them. Certainly we are a sufficiently comical invention, we humans.

Sincerely Yours,

S. L. CLEMENS.

Mark Twain's own books were always being excommunicated by some librarian, and the matter never failed to invite the attention and amusement of the press, and the indignation of many correspondents. Usually the books were Tom Sawyer and Huck Finn, the morals of which were not regarded as wholly exemplary. But in 1907 a small library, in a very small town, attained a day's national notoriety by putting the ban on Eve's Diary, not so much on account of its text as for the chaste and exquisite illustrations by Lester Ralph. When the reporters came in a troop to learn about it, the author said: "I believe this time the trouble is mainly with the pictures. I did not draw them. I wish I had—they are so beautiful."

Just at this time, Dr. William Lyon Phelps, of Yale, was giving a literary talk to the Teachers' Club, of Hartford, dwelling on the superlative value of Mark Twain's writings for readers old and young. Mrs. F. G. Whitmore, an old Hartford friend, wrote Clemens of the things that Phelps had said, as consolation for Eve's latest banishment. This gave him a chance to add something to what he had said to the reporters.

To Mrs. Whitmore, in Hartford:

Feb. 7, 1907.

DEAR MRS. WHITMORE,—But the truth is, that when a Library expels a book of mine and leaves an unexpurgated Bible lying around where unprotected youth and age can get hold of it, the deep unconscious irony of it delights me and doesn't anger me. But even if it angered me such words as those of Professor Phelps would take the sting all out. Nobody attaches weight to the freaks of the Charlton Library, but when a man like Phelps speaks, the world gives attention. Some day I hope to meet him and thank him for his courage for saying those things out in public. Custom is, to think a handsome thing in private but tame it down in the utterance.

I hope you are all well and happy; and thereto I add my love.

Sincerely yours,

S. L. CLEMENS.

In May, 1907, Mark Twain was invited to England to receive from Oxford the degree of Literary Doctor. It was an honor that came to him as a sort of laurel crown at the end of a great career, and gratified him exceedingly. To Moberly Bell, of the London Times, he expressed his appreciation. Bell had been over in April and Clemens believed him concerned in the matter.

To Moberly Bell, in London:

21 FIFTH AVENUE, May 3, '07

DEAR MR. BELL,—Your hand is in it! and you have my best thanks. Although I wouldn't cross an ocean again for the price of the ship that carried me, I am glad to do it for an Oxford degree. I shall plan to sail for England a shade before the middle of June, so that I can have a few days in London before the 26th.

Sincerely,

S. L. CLEMENS.

He had taken a house at Tuxedo for the summer, desiring to be near New York City, and in the next letter he writes Mr. Rogers concerning his London plans. We discover, also, in this letter that he has begun work on the Redding home and the cost is to come entirely out of the autobiographical chapters then running in the North American Review. It may be of passing interest to note here that he had the usual house-builder's fortune. He received thirty thousand dollars for the chapters; the house cost him nearly double that amount.

To H. H. Rogers, in New York:

TUXEDO PARK,

May 29, '07.

DEAR ADMIRAL,—Why hang it, I am not going to see you and Mrs. Rogers at all in England! It is a great disappointment. I leave there a month from now—June 29. No, I shall see you; for by your itinerary you are most likely to come to London June 21st or along there. So that is very good and satisfactory. I have declined all engagements but two—Whitelaw Reid (dinner) June 21, and the Pilgrims (lunch), June 25. The Oxford ceremony is June 26. I have paid my return passage in the Minne-something, but it is just possible that I may want to stay in England a week or two longer—I can't tell, yet. I do very much want to meet up with the boys for the last time.

I have signed the contract for the building of the house on my Connecticut farm and specified the cost limit, and work has been begun. The cost has to all come out of a year's instalments of Autobiography in the N. A. Review.

Clara, is winning her way to success and distinction with sure and steady strides. By all accounts she is singing like a bird, and is not afraid on the concert stage any more.

Tuxedo is a charming place; I think it hasn't its equal anywhere.

Very best wishes to you both.

S. L. C.

The story of Mark Twain's extraordinary reception and triumph in England has been told.—[Mark Twain; A Biography, chaps. cclvi-cclix]—It was, in fact, the crowning glory of his career. Perhaps one of the most satisfactory incidents of his sojourn was a dinner given to him by the staff of Punch, in the historic offices at 10 Bouverie Street where no other foreign visitor had been thus honored—a notable distinction. When the dinner ended, little joy Agnew, daughter of the chief editor, entered and presented to the chief guest the original drawing of a cartoon by Bernard Partridge, which had appeared on the front page of Punch. In this picture the presiding genius of the paper is offering to Mark Twain health, long life, and happiness from "The Punch Bowl."

A short time after his return to America he received a pretty childish letter from little Miss Agnew acknowledging a photograph he had sent her, and giving a list of her pets and occupations. Such a letter always delighted Mark Twain, and his pleasure in this one is reflected in his reply.

To Miss Joy Agnew, in London:

TUXEDO PARK, NEW YORK.

Unto you greetings and salutation and worship, you dear, sweet little rightly-named Joy! I can see you now almost as vividly as I saw you that night when you sat flashing and beaming upon those sombre swallow-tails.

"Fair as a star when only one

Is shining in the sky."

Oh, you were indeed the only one—there wasn't even the remotest chance of competition with you, dear! Ah, you are a decoration, you little witch!

The idea of your house going to the wanton expense of a flower garden!—aren't you enough? And what do you want to go and discourage the other flowers for? Is that the right spirit? is it considerate? is it kind? How do you suppose they feel when you come around—looking the way you look? And you so pink and sweet and dainty and lovely and supernatural? Why, it makes them feel embarrassed and artificial, of course; and in my opinion it is just as pathetic as it can be. Now then you want to reform—dear—and do right.

Well certainly you are well off, Joy:

3 bantams;

3 goldfish;

3 doves;

6 canaries;

2 dogs;

1 cat;

All you need, now, to be permanently beyond the reach of want, is one more dog—just one more good, gentle, high principled, affectionate, loyal dog who wouldn't want any nobler service than the golden privilege of lying at your door, nights, and biting everything that came along—and I am that very one, and ready to come at the dropping of a hat.

Do you think you could convey my love and thanks to your "daddy" and Owen Seaman and those other oppressed and down-trodden subjects of yours, you darling small tyrant?

On my knees! These—with the kiss of fealty from your other subject—

MARK TWAIN

Elinor Glyn, author of Three Weeks and other erotic tales, was in America that winter and asked permission to call on Mark Twain. An appointment was made and Clemens discussed with her, for an hour or more, those crucial phases of life which have made living a complex problem since the days of Eve in Eden. Mrs. Glyn had never before heard anything like Mark Twain's wonderful talk, and she was anxious to print their interview. She wrote what she could remember of it and sent it to him for approval. If his conversation had been frank, his refusal was hardly less so.

To Mrs. Elinor Glyn, in New York:

Jan. 22, '08.

DEAR MRS. GLYN, It reads pretty poorly—I get the sense of it, but it is a poor literary job; however, it would have to be that because nobody can be reported even approximately, except by a stenographer. Approximations, synopsized speeches, translated poems, artificial flowers and chromos all have a sort of value, but it is small. If you had put upon paper what I really said it would have wrecked your type-machine. I said some fetid, over-vigorous things, but that was because it was a confidential conversation. I said nothing for print. My own report of the same conversation reads like Satan roasting a Sunday school. It, and certain other readable chapters of my autobiography will not be published until all the Clemens family are dead—dead and correspondingly indifferent. They were written to entertain me, not the rest of the world. I am not here to do good—at least not to do it intentionally. You must pardon me for dictating this letter; I am sick a-bed and not feeling as well as I might.

Sincerely Yours,

S. L. CLEMENS.

Among the cultured men of England Mark Twain had no greater admirer, or warmer friend, than Andrew Lang. They were at one on most literary subjects, and especially so in their admiration of the life and character of Joan of Arc. Both had written of her, and both held her to be something almost more than mortal. When, therefore, Anatole France published his exhaustive biography of the maid of Domremy, a book in which he followed, with exaggerated minuteness and innumerable footnotes, every step of Joan's physical career at the expense of her spiritual life, which he was inclined to cheapen, Lang wrote feelingly, and with some contempt, of the performance, inviting the author of the Personal Recollections to come to the rescue of their heroine. "Compare every one of his statements with the passages he cites from authorities, and make him the laughter of the world" he wrote. "If you are lazy about comparing I can make you a complete set of what the authorities say, and of what this amazing novelist says that they say. When I tell you that he thinks the Epiphany (January 6, Twelfth Night) is December 25th—Christmas Day-you begin to see what an egregious ass he is. Treat him like Dowden, and oblige"—a reference to Mark Twain's defense of Harriet Shelley, in which he had heaped ridicule on Dowden's Life of the Poet—a masterly performance; one of the best that ever came from Mark Twain's pen.

Lang's suggestion would seem to have been a welcome one.

To Andrew Lang, in London:

NEW YORK, April 25, 1908.

DEAR MR. LANG,—I haven't seen the book nor any review of it, but only not very-understandable references to it—of a sort which discomforted me, but of course set my interest on fire. I don't want to have to read it in French—I should lose the nice shades, and should do a lot of gross misinterpreting, too. But there'll be a translation soon, nicht wahr? I will wait for it. I note with joy that you say: "If you are lazy about comparing, (which I most certainly am), I can make you a complete set of what the authorities say, and of what this amazing novelist says that they say."

Ah, do it for me! Then I will attempt the article, and (if I succeed in doing it to my satisfaction,) will publish it. It is long since I touched a pen (3 1/2 years), and I was intending to continue this happy holiday to the gallows, but—there are things that could beguile me to break this blessed Sabbath.

Yours very sincerely,

S. L. CLEMENS.

Certainly it is an interesting fact that an Englishman—one of the race that burned Joan—should feel moved to defend her memory against the top-heavy perversions of a distinguished French author.

But Lang seems never to have sent the notes. The copying would have been a tremendous task, and perhaps he never found the time for it. We may regret to-day that he did not, for Mark Twain's article on the French author's Joan would have been at least unique.

Samuel Clemens could never accustom himself to the loss of his wife. From the time of her death, marriage-which had brought him his greatest joy in life-presented itself to him always with the thought of bereavement, waiting somewhere just behind. The news of an approaching wedding saddened him and there was nearly always a somber tinge in his congratulations, of which the following to a dear friend is an example:

To Father Fitz-Simon, in Washington:

June 5, '08.

DEAR FATHER FITZ-SIMON,—Marriage—yes, it is the supreme felicity of life, I concede it. And it is also the supreme tragedy of life. The deeper the love the surer the tragedy. And the more disconsolating when it comes.

And so I congratulate you. Not perfunctorily, not lukewarmly, but with a fervency and fire that no word in the dictionary is strong enough to convey.

And in the same breath and with the same depth and sincerity, I grieve for you. Not for both of you and not for the one that shall go first, but for the one that is fated to be left behind. For that one there is no recompense.—For that one no recompense is possible.

There are times—thousands of times—when I can expose the half of my mind, and conceal the other half, but in the matter of the tragedy of marriage I feel too deeply for that, and I have to bleed it all out or shut it all in. And so you must consider what I have been through, and am passing through and be charitable with me.

Make the most of the sunshine! and I hope it will last long—ever so long.

I do not really want to be present; yet for friendship's sake and because I honor you so, I would be there if I could.

Most sincerely your friend,

S. L. CLEMENS.

The new home at Redding was completed in the spring of 1908, and on the 18th of June, when it was entirely fitted and furnished, Mark Twain entered it for the first time. He had never even seen the place nor carefully examined plans which John Howells had made for his house. He preferred the surprise of it, and the general avoidance of detail. That he was satisfied with the result will be seen in his letters. He named it at first "Innocence at Home"; later changing this title to "Stormfield."

The letter which follows is an acknowledgment of an interesting souvenir from the battle-field of Tewksbury (1471), and some relics of the Cavalier and Roundhead Regiments encamped at Tewksbury in 1643.

To an English admirer:

INNOCENCE AT HOME, REDDING, CONNECTICUT,

Aug. 15, '08.

DEAR SIR,—I highly prize the pipes, and shall intimate to people that "Raleigh" smoked them, and doubtless he did. After a little practice I shall be able to go further and say he did; they will then be the most interesting features of my library's decorations. The Horse-shoe is attracting a good deal of attention, because I have intimated that the conqueror's horse cast it; it will attract more when I get my hand in and say he cast it, I thank you for the pipes and the shoe; and also for the official guide, which I read through at a single sitting. If a person should say that about a book of mine I should regard it as good evidence of the book's interest.

Very truly yours,

S. L. CLEMENS.

In his philosophy, What Is Man?, and now and again in his other writings, we find Mark Twain giving small credit to the human mind as an originator of ideas. The most original writer of his time, he took no credit for pure invention and allowed none to others. The mind, he declared, adapted, consciously or unconsciously; it did not create. In a letter which follows he elucidates this doctrine. The reference in it to the "captain" and to the kerosene, as the reader may remember, have to do with Captain "Hurricane" Jones and his theory of the miracles of "Isaac and of the prophets of Baal," as expounded in Some Rambling Notes of an Idle Excursion.

By a trick of memory Clemens gives The Little Duke as his suggestion for The Prince and the Pauper; he should have written The Prince and the Page, by the same author.

To Rev. F. Y. Christ, in New York:

REDDING, CONN., Aug., '08.

DEAR SIR,—You say "I often owe my best sermons to a suggestion received in reading or from other exterior sources." Your remark is not quite in accordance with the facts. We must change it to—"I owe all my thoughts, sermons and ideas to suggestions received from sources outside of myself." The simplified English of this proposition is—"No man's brains ever originated an idea." It is an astonishing thing that after all these ages the world goes on thinking the human brain machinery can originate a thought.

It can't. It never has done it. In all cases, little and big, the thought is born of a suggestion; and in all cases the suggestions come to the brain from the outside. The brain never acts except from exterior impulse.

A man can satisfy himself of the truth of this by a single process,—let him examine every idea that occurs to him in an hour; a day; in a week—in a lifetime if he please. He will always find that an outside something suggested the thought, something which he saw with his eyes or heard with his ears or perceived by his touch—not necessarily to-day, nor yesterday, nor last year, nor twenty years ago, but sometime or other. Usually the source of the suggestion is immediately traceable, but sometimes it isn't.

However, if you will examine every thought that occurs to you for the next two days, you will find that in at least nine cases out of ten you can put your finger on the outside suggestion—And that ought to convince you that No. 10 had that source too, although you cannot at present hunt it down and find it.

The idea of writing to me would have had to wait a long time if it waited until your brain originated it. It was born of an outside suggestion—Sir Thomas and my old Captain.

The hypnotist thinks he has invented a new thing—suggestion. This is very sad. I don't know where my captain got his kerosene idea. (It was forty-one years ago, and he is long ago dead.) But I know that it didn't originate in his head, but it was born from a suggestion from the outside.

Yesterday a guest said, "How did you come to think of writing 'The Prince and the Pauper?'" I didn't. The thought came to me from the outside—suggested by that pleasant and picturesque little history-book, Charlotte M. Yonge's "Little Duke," I doubt if Mrs. Burnett knows whence came to her the suggestion to write "Little Lord Fauntleroy," but I know; it came to her from reading "The Prince and the Pauper." In all my life I have never originated an idea, and neither has she, nor anybody else.

Man's mind is a clever machine, and can work up materials into ingenious fancies and ideas, but it can't create the material; none but the gods can do that. In Sweden I saw a vast machine receive a block of wood, and turn it into marketable matches in two minutes. It could do everything but make the wood. That is the kind of machine the human mind is. Maybe this is not a large compliment, but it is all I can afford.....

Your friend and well-wisher

S. L. CLEMENS.

To Mrs. H. H. Rogers, in Fair Hawn, Mass.:

REDDING, CONN, Aug. 12, 1908.

DEAR MRS. ROGERS, I believe I am the wellest man on the planet to-day, and good for a trip to Fair Haven (which I discussed with the Captain of the New Bedford boat, who pleasantly accosted me in the Grand Central August 5) but the doctor came up from New York day before yesterday, and gave positive orders that I must not stir from here before frost. It is because

I was threatened with a swoon, 10 or 12 days ago, and went to New York a day or two later to attend my nephew's funeral and got horribly exhausted by the heat and came back here and had a bilious collapse. In 24 hours I was as sound as a nut again, but nobody believes it but me.

This is a prodigiously satisfactory place, and I am so glad I don't have to go back to the turmoil and rush of New York. The house stands high and the horizons are wide, yet the seclusion is perfect. The nearest public road is half a mile away, so there is nobody to look in, and I don't have to wear clothes if I don't want to. I have been down stairs in night-gown and slippers a couple of hours, and have been photographed in that costume; but I will dress, now, and behave myself.

That doctor had half an idea that there is something the matter with my brain... Doctors do know so little and they do charge so much for it. I wish Henry Rogers would come here, and I wish you would come with him. You can't rest in that crowded place, but you could rest here, for sure! I would learn bridge, and entertain you, and rob you.

With love to you both,

Ever yours,

S. L. C.

In the foregoing letter we get the first intimation of Mark Twain's failing health. The nephew who had died was Samuel E. Moffett, son of Pamela Clemens. Moffett, who was a distinguished journalist—an editorial writer on Collier's Weekly, a man beloved by all who knew him—had been drowned in the surf off the Jersey beach.

To W. D. Howells, Kittery Point, Maine:

Aug. 12, '08.

DEAR HOWELLS,—Won't you and Mrs. Howells and Mildred come

and give us as many days as you can spare, and examine John's triumph? It is the most satisfactory house I am acquainted with, and the most satisfactorily situated.

But it is no place to work in, because one is outside of it all the time, while the sun and the moon are on duty. Outside of it in the loggia, where the breezes blow and the tall arches divide up the scenery and frame it.

It's a ghastly long distance to come, and I wouldn't travel such a distance to see anything short of a memorial museum, but if you can't come now you can at least come later when you return to New York, for the journey will be only an hour and a half per express-train. Things are gradually and steadily taking shape inside the house, and nature is taking care of the outside in her ingenious and wonderful fashion—and she is competent and asks no help and gets none. I have retired from New York for good, I have retired from labor for good, I have dismissed my stenographer and have entered upon a holiday whose other end is in the cemetery.

Yours ever,

MARK.

From a gentleman in Buffalo Clemens one day received a letter inclosing an incompleted list of the world's "One Hundred Greatest Men," men who had exerted "the largest visible influence on the life and activities of the race." The writer asked that Mark Twain examine the list and suggest names, adding "would you include Jesus, as the founder of Christianity, in the list?"

To the list of statesmen Clemens added the name of Thomas Paine; to the list of inventors, Edison and Alexander Graham Bell. The question he answered in detail.

To ———, Buffalo, N. Y.

Private. REDDING, CONN, Aug. 28, '08.

DEAR SIR,—By "private," I mean don't print any remarks of mine.

....

I like your list.

The "largest visible influence."

These terms require you to add Jesus. And they doubly and trebly require you to add Satan. From A.D. 350 to A.D. 1850 these gentlemen exercised a vaster influence over a fifth part of the human race than was exercised over that fraction of the race by all other influences combined. Ninety-nine hundredths of this influence proceeded from Satan, the remaining fraction of it from Jesus. During those 1500 years the fear of Satan and Hell made 99 Christians where love of God and Heaven landed one. During those 1500 years, Satan's influence was worth very nearly a hundred times as much to the business as was the influence of all the rest of the Holy Family put together.

You have asked me a question, and I have answered it seriously and sincerely. You have put in Buddha—a god, with a following, at one time, greater than Jesus ever had: a god with perhaps a little better evidence of his godship than that which is offered for Jesus's. How then, in fairness, can you leave Jesus out? And if you put him in, how can you logically leave Satan out? Thunder is good, thunder is impressive; but it is the lightning that does the work.

Very truly yours,

S. L. CLEMENS.

The "Children's Theatre" of the next letter was an institution of the New York East Side in which Mark Twain was deeply interested. The children were most, if not all, of Hebrew parentage, and the performances they gave, under the direction of Alice M. Herts, were really remarkable. It seemed a pity that lack of funds should have brought this excellent educational venture to an untimely end.

The following letter was in reply to one inclosing a newspaper clipping reporting a performance of The Prince and the Pauper, given by Chicago school children.

To Mrs. Hookway, in Chicago:

Sept., 1908.

DEAR MRS. HOOKWAY,—Although I am full of the spirit of work this morning, a rarity with me lately—I must steal a moment or two for a word in person: for I have been reading the eloquent account in the Record-Herald and am pleasurably stirred, to my deepest deeps. The reading brings vividly back to me my pet and pride. The Children's Theatre of the East side, New York. And it supports and re-affirms what I have so often and strenuously said in public that a children's theatre is easily the most valuable adjunct that any educational institution for the young can have, and that no otherwise good school is complete without it.

It is much the most effective teacher of morals and promoter of good conduct that the ingenuity of man has yet devised, for the reason that its lessons are not taught wearily by book and by dreary homily, but by visible and enthusing action; and they go straight to the heart, which is the rightest of right places for them. Book morals often get no further than the intellect, if they even get that far on their spectral and shadowy pilgrimage: but when they travel from a Children's Theatre they do not stop permanently at that halfway house, but go on home.

The children's theatre is the only teacher of morals and conduct and high ideals that never bores the pupil, but always leaves him sorry when the lesson is over. And as for history, no other teacher is for a moment comparable to it: no other can make the dead heroes of the world rise up and shake the dust of the ages from their bones and live and move and breathe and speak and be real to the looker and listener: no other can make the study of the lives and times of the illustrious dead a delight, a splendid interest, a passion; and no other can paint a history-lesson in colors that will stay, and stay, and never fade.

It is my conviction that the children's theatre is one of the very, very great inventions of the twentieth century; and that its vast educational value—now but dimly perceived and but vaguely understood—will presently come to be recognized. By the article which I have been reading I find the same things happening in the Howland School that we have become familiar with in our Children's Theatre (of which I am President, and sufficiently vain of the distinction.) These things among others;

1. The educating history-study does not stop with the little players, but the whole school catches the infection and revels in it.

2. And it doesn't even stop there; the children carry it home and infect the family with it—even the parents and grandparents; and the whole household fall to studying history, and bygone manners and customs and costumes with eager interest. And this interest is carried along to the studying of costumes in old book-plates; and beyond that to the selecting of fabrics and the making of clothes. Hundreds of our children learn, the plays by listening without book, and by making notes; then the listener goes home and plays the piece—all the parts! to the family. And the family are glad and proud; glad to listen to the explanations and analyses, glad to learn, glad to be lifted to planes above their dreary workaday lives. Our children's theatre is educating 7,000 children—and their families. When we put on a play of Shakespeare they fall to studying it diligently; so that they may be qualified to enjoy it to the limit when the piece is staged.

3. Your Howland School children do the construction-work, stage-decorations, etc. That is our way too. Our young folks do everything that is needed by the theatre, with their own hands; scene-designing, scene-painting, gas-fitting, electric work, costume-designing—costume making, everything

and all things indeed—and their orchestra and its leader are from their own ranks.

The article which I have been reading, says—speaking of the historical play produced by the pupils of the Howland School—

"The question naturally arises, What has this drama done for those who so enthusiastically took part?—The touching story has made a year out of the Past live for the children as could no chronology or bald statement of historical events; it has cultivated the fancy and given to the imagination strength and purity; work in composition has ceased to be drudgery, for when all other themes fall flat a subject dealing with some aspect of the drama presented never fails to arouse interest and a rapid pushing of pens over paper."

That is entirely true. The interest is not confined to the drama's story, it spreads out all around the period of the story, and gives to all the outlying and unrelated happenings of that period a fascinating interest—an interest which does not fade out with the years, but remains always fresh, always inspiring, always welcome. History-facts dug by the job, with sweat and tears out of a dry and spiritless text-book—but never mind, all who have suffered know what that is...

I remain, dear madam,

Sincerely yours,

S. L. CLEMENS.

Mark Twain had a special fondness for cats. As a boy he always owned one and it generally had a seat beside him at the table. There were cats at Quarry Farm and at Hartford, and in the house at Redding there was a gray mother-cat named Tammany, of which he was especially fond. Kittens capering about were his chief delight. In a letter to a Chicago woman he tells how those of Tammany assisted at his favorite game.

To Mrs. Mabel Larkin Patterson, in Chicago:

REDDING, CONNECTICUT,

Oct. 2, '08.

DEAR MRS. PATTERSON,—The contents of your letter are very pleasant and very welcome, and I thank you for them, sincerely. If I can find a photograph of my "Tammany" and her kittens, I will enclose it in this.

One of them likes to be crammed into a corner-pocket of the billiard table—which he fits as snugly as does a finger in a glove and then he watches the game (and obstructs it) by the hour, and spoils many a shot by putting out his paw and changing the direction of a passing ball. Whenever a ball is in his arms, or so close to him that it cannot be played upon without risk of hurting him, the player is privileged to remove it to anyone of the 3 spots that chances to be vacant.

Ah, no, my lecturing days are over for good and all.

Sincerely yours,

S. L. CLEMENS.

The letter to Howells which follows was written a short time before the passage of the copyright extension bill, which rendered Mark Twain's new plan, here mentioned, unneeded—at least for the time.

To W. D. Howells, in New York:

Monday, Oct. 26, '08.

Oh, I say! Where are you hiding, and why are you hiding? You promised to come here and you didn't keep your word. (This sounds like astonishment—but don't be misled by that.)

Come, fire up again on your fiction-mill and give us another good promise. And this time keep it—for it is your turn to be astonished. Come and stay as long as you possibly can. I invented a new copyright extension scheme last Friday, and sat up all night arranging its details. It will interest you. Yesterday I got it down on paper in as compact a form as I could. Harvey and I have examined the scheme, and to-morrow or next day he will send me a couple of copyright-experts to arrange about getting certain statistics for me.

Authors, publishers and the public have always been damaged by the copyright laws. The proposed amendment will advantage all three—the public most of all. I think Congress will pass it and settle the vexed question permanently.

I shall need your assent and the assent of about a dozen other authors. Also the assent of all the large firms of the 300 publishers. These authors and publishers will furnish said assent I am sure. Not even the pirates will be able to furnish a serious objection, I think.

Come along. This place seemed at its best when all around was summer-green; later it seemed at its best when all around was burning with the autumn splendors; and now once more it seems at its best, with the trees naked and the ground a painter's palette.

Yours ever,

MARK.

Clemens was a great admirer of the sea stories of W. W. Jacobs and generally kept one or more of this author's volumes in reach of his bed, where most of his reading was done. The acknowledgment that follows was sent when he had finished Salthaven.

To W. W. Jacobs, in England:

REDDING, CONN,

Oct. 28, '08.

DEAR MR. JACOBS,—It has a delightful look. I will not venture to say how delightful, because the words would sound extravagant, and would thereby lose some of their strength and to that degree misrepresent me. It is my conviction that Dialstone Lane holds the supremacy over all purely humorous books in our language, but I feel about Salthaven as the Cape Cod poet feels about Simon Hanks:

"The Lord knows all things, great and small,

With doubt he's not perplexed:

'Tis Him alone that knows it all

But Simon Hanks comes next."

The poet was moved by envy and malice and jealousy, but I am not: I place Salthaven close up next to Dialstone because I think it has a fair and honest right to that high position. I have kept the other book moving; I shall begin to hand this one around now.

And many thanks to you for remembering me.

This house is out in the solitudes of the woods and the hills, an hour and a half from New York, and I mean to stay in it winter and summer the rest of my days. I beg you to come and help occupy it a few days the next time you visit the U.S.

Sincerely yours,

S. L. CLEMENS.

One of the attractions of Stormfield was a beautiful mantel in the billiard room, presented by the Hawaiian Promotion Committee. It had not arrived when the rest of the house was completed, but came in time to be set in place early in the morning of the owner's seventy-third birthday. It was made of a variety of Hawaiian woods, and was the work of a native carver, F. M. Otremba. Clemens was deeply touched by the offering from those "western isles"—the memory of which was always so sweet to him.

To Mr. Wood, in Hawaii:

Nov. 30, '08.

DEAR MR. WOOD,—The beautiful mantel was put in its place an hour ago, and its friendly "Aloha" was the first uttered greeting my 73rd birthday received. It is rich in color, rich in quality, and rich in decoration, therefore it exactly harmonizes with the taste for such things which was born in me and which I have seldom been able to indulge to my content. It will be a great pleasure to me, daily renewed, to have under my eye this lovely reminder of the loveliest fleet of islands that lies anchored in any ocean, and I beg to thank the Committee for providing me that pleasure.

Sincerely Yours,

S. L. CLEMENS.

XLVII. LETTERS, 1909. TO HOWELLS AND OTHERS. LIFE AT STORMFIELD. COPYRIGHT EXTENSION. DEATH OF JEAN CLEMENS

Clemens remained at Stormfield all that winter. New York was sixty miles away and he did not often care to make the journey. He was constantly invited to this or that public gathering, or private party, but such affairs had lost interest for him. He preferred the quiet of his luxurious home with its beautiful outlook, while for entertainment he found the billiard afternoons sufficient. Guests came from the city, now and again, for week-end visits, and if he ever was restless or lonely he did not show it.

Among the invitations that came was one from General O. O. Howard asking him to preside at a meeting to raise an endowment fund for a Lincoln Memorial University at Cumberland Gap, Tennessee. Closing his letter, General Howard said, "Never mind if you did fight on the other side."

To General O. O. Howard:

STORMFIELD, REDDING, CONNECTICUT,

Jan, 12, '09.

DEAR GENERAL HOWARD,—You pay me a most gratifying compliment in asking me to preside, and it causes me very real regret that I am obliged to decline, for the object of the meeting appeals strongly to me, since that object is to aid in raising the $500,000 Endowment Fund for

Lincoln Memorial University. The Endowment Fund will be the most fitting of all the memorials the country will dedicate to the memory of Lincoln, serving, as it will, to uplift his very own people.

I hope you will meet with complete success, and I am sorry I cannot be there to witness it and help you rejoice. But I am older than people think, and besides I live away out in the country and never stir from home, except at geological intervals, to fill left-over engagements in mesozoic times when I was younger and indiscreeter.

You ought not to say sarcastic things about my "fighting on the other side." General Grant did not act like that. General Grant paid me compliments. He bracketed me with Zenophon—it is there in his Memoirs for anybody to read. He said if all the confederate soldiers had followed my example and adopted my military arts he could never have caught enough of them in a bunch to inconvenience the Rebellion. General Grant was a fair man, and recognized my worth; but you are prejudiced, and you have hurt my feelings.

But I have an affection for you, anyway.

MARK TWAIN.

One of Mark Twain's friends was Henniker-Heaton, the so-called "Father of Penny Postage" between England and America. When, after long years of effort, he succeeded in getting the rate established, he at once bent his energies in the direction of cheap cable service and a letter from him came one day to Stormfield concerning his new plans. This letter happened to be over-weight, which gave Mark Twain a chance for some amusing exaggerations at his expense.

To Henniker-Heaton, in London:

STORMFIELD, REDDING, CONNECTICUT,

Jan. 18, 1909.

DEAR HENNIKER-HEATON,—I do hope you will succeed to your heart's desire in your cheap-cablegram campaign, and I feel sure you will. Indeed your cheap-postage victory, achieved in spite of a quarter-century of determined opposition, is good and rational prophecy that you will. Wireless, not being as yet imprisoned in a Chinese wall of private cash and high-placed and formidable influence, will come to your aid and make your new campaign briefer and easier than the other one was.

Now then, after uttering my serious word, am I privileged to be frivolous for a moment? When you shall have achieved cheap telegraphy, are you going to employ it for just your own selfish profit and other people's pecuniary damage, the way you are doing with your cheap postage? You get letter-postage reduced to 2 cents an ounce, then you mail me a 4-ounce letter with a 2-cent stamp on it, and I have to pay the extra freight at this end of the line. I return your envelope for inspection. Look at it. Stamped in one place is a vast "T," and under it the figures "40," and under those figures appears an "L," a sinister and suspicious and mysterious L. In another place, stamped within a circle, in offensively large capitals, you find the words "DUE 8 CENTS." Finally, in the midst of a desert space up nor-noreastard from that circle you find a figure "3" of quite unnecessarily aggressive and insolent magnitude—and done with a blue pencil, so as to be as conspicuous as possible. I inquired about these strange signs and symbols of the postman. He said they were P. O. Department signals for his instruction.

"Instruction for what?"

"To get extra postage."

"Is it so? Explain. Tell me about the large T and the 40.

"It's short for Take 40—or as we postmen say, grab 40"

"Go on, please, while I think up some words to swear with."

"Due 8 means, grab 8 more."

"Continue."

"The blue-pencil 3 was an afterthought. There aren't any stamps for afterthoughts; the sums vary, according to inspiration, and they whirl in the one that suggests itself at the last moment. Sometimes they go several times higher than this one. This one only means hog 3 cents more. And so if you've got 51 cents about you, or can borrow it—"

"Tell me: who gets this corruption?"

"Half of it goes to the man in England who ships the letter on short postage, and the other half goes to the P.O.D. to protect cheap postage from inaugurating a deficit."

"_______________________."

"I can't blame you; I would say it myself in your place, if these ladies were not present. But you see I'm only obeying orders, I can't help myself."

"Oh, I know it; I'm not blaming you. Finally, what does that L stand for?"

"Get the money, or give him L. It's English, you know."

"Take it and go. It's the last cent I've got in the world—."

After seeing the Oxford pageant file by the grand stand, picture after picture, splendor after splendor, three thousand five hundred strong, the most moving and beautiful and impressive and historically-instructive show conceivable, you are not to think I would miss the London pageant of next year, with its shining host of 15,000 historical English men and women dug from the misty books of all the vanished ages and marching in the light of the sun—all alive, and looking just as they were used to look! Mr. Lascelles spent yesterday here on the farm, and told me all about it. I shall be in the middle of my 75th year then, and interested in pageants for personal and prospective reasons.

I beg you to give my best thanks to the Bath Club for the offer of its hospitalities, but I shall not be able to take advantage of it, because I am to be a guest in a private house during my stay in London.

Sincerely yours,

S. L. CLEMENS.

It was in 1907 that Clemens had seen the Oxford Pageant—during the week when he had been awarded his doctor's degree. It gave him the greatest delight, and he fully expected to see the next one, planned for 1910.

In the letter to Howells which follows we get another glimpse of Mark Twain's philosophy of man, the irresponsible machine.

To W. D. Howells, in New York:

STORMFIELD, REDDING, CONN.,

Jan. 18, '09.

DEAR HOWELLS,—I have to write a line, lazy as I am, to say how your Poe article delighted me; and to say that I am in agreement with substantially all you say about his literature. To me his prose is unreadable—like Jane Austin's. No, there is a difference. I could read his prose on salary, but not Jane's. Jane is entirely impossible. It seems a great pity that they allowed her to die a natural death.

Another thing: you grant that God and circumstances sinned against Poe, but you also grant that he sinned against himself—a thing which he couldn't do and didn't do.

It is lively up here now. I wish you could come.

Yrs ever,

MARK

To W. D. Howells, in New York:

STORMFIELD, REDDING, CONNECTICUT,

3 in the morning, Apl. 17, '09.

[Written with pencil].

My pen has gone dry and the ink is out of reach. Howells, Did you write me day-before-day before yesterday, or did I dream it? In my mind's eye I most vividly see your hand-write on a square blue envelop in the mailpile. I have hunted the house over, but there is no such letter. Was it an illusion?

I am reading Lowell's letter, and smoking. I woke an hour ago and am reading to keep from wasting the time. On page 305, vol. I. I have just margined a note:

"Young friend! I like that! You ought to see him now."

It seemed startlingly strange to hear a person call you young. It was a brick out of a blue sky, and knocked me groggy for a moment. Ah me, the pathos of it is, that we were young then. And he—why, so was he, but he didn't know it. He didn't even know it 9 years later, when we saw him approaching and you warned me, saying, "Don't say anything about age—he has just turned fifty, and thinks he is old and broods over it."

[Well, Clara did sing! And you wrote her a dear letter.]

Time to go to sleep.

Yours ever,

MARK.

To Daniel Kiefer:

[No date.]

DANL KIEFER ESQ. DEAR SIR,—I should be far from willing to have a political party named after me.

I would not be willing to belong to a party which allowed its members to have political aspirations or to push friends forward for political preferment.

Yours very truly,

S. L. CLEMENS.

The copyright extension, for which the author had been working so long, was granted by Congress in 1909, largely as the result of that afternoon in Washington when Mark Twain had "received" in "Uncle Joe" Cannon's private room, and preached the gospel of copyright until the daylight faded and the rest of the Capitol grew still. Champ Clark was the last to linger that day and they had talked far into the dusk. Clark was powerful, and had fathered the bill. Now he wrote to know if it was satisfactory.

To Champ Clark, in Washington:

STORMFIELD, REDDING, CONN., June 5, '09.

DEAR CHAMP CLARK—Is the new copyright law acceptable to me? Emphatically, yes! Clark, it is the only sane, and clearly defined, and just and righteous copyright law that has ever existed in the United States. Whosoever will compare it with its predecessors will have no trouble in arriving at that decision.

The bill which was before the committee two years ago when I was down there was the most stupefying jumble of conflicting and apparently irreconcilable interests that was ever seen; and we all said "the case is hopeless, absolutely hopeless—out of this chaos nothing can be built." But we were in error; out of that chaotic mass this excellent bill has been instructed; the warring interests have been reconciled, and the result is as comely and substantial a legislative edifice as lifts its domes and towers and protective lightning rods out of the statute book, I think. When I think of that other bill, which even the Deity couldn't understand, and of this one which even I can understand, I take off my hat to the man or men who devised this one. Was it R. U. Johnson? Was it the Author's League? Was it both together? I don't know, but I take off my hat, anyway. Johnson has written a valuable article about the new law—I enclose it.

At last—at last and for the first time in copyright history we are ahead of England! Ahead of her in two ways: by length of time and by fairness to all interests concerned. Does this sound like shouting? Then I must modify it: all we possessed of copyright-justice before the fourth of last March we owed to England's initiative.

Truly Yours,

S. L. CLEMENS.

Because Mark Twain amused himself with certain aspects of Christian Science, and was critical of Mrs. Eddy, there grew up a wide impression that he jeered at the theory of mental healing; when, as a matter of fact, he was one of its earliest converts, and never lost faith in its power. The letter which follows is an excellent exposition of his attitude toward the institution of Christian Science and the founder of the church in America.

To J. Wylie Smith, Glasgow, Scotland:

"STORMFIELD," August 7, 1909

DEAR SIR,—My view of the matter has not changed. To wit, that Christian Science is valuable; that it has just the same value now that it had when Mrs. Eddy stole it from Quimby; that its healing principle (its most valuable asset) possesses the same force now that it possessed a million years ago before Quimby was born; that Mrs. Eddy... organized that force, and is entitled to high credit for that. Then, with a splendid sagacity she hitched it to... a religion, the surest of all ways to secure friends for it, and support. In a fine and lofty way—figuratively speaking—it was a tramp stealing a ride on the lightning express. Ah, how did that ignorant village-born peasant woman know the human being so well? She has no more intellect than a tadpole—until it comes to business then she is a marvel! Am I sorry I wrote the book? Most certainly not. You say you have 500 (converts) in Glasgow. Fifty years from now, your posterity will not count them by the hundred, but by the thousand. I feel absolutely sure of this.

Very truly yours,

S. L. CLEMENS.

Clemens wrote very little for publication that year, but he enjoyed writing for his own amusement, setting down the things that boiled, or bubbled, within him: mainly chapters on the inconsistencies of human deportment, human superstition and human creeds. The "Letters from the Earth" referred to in the following, were supposed to have been written by an immortal visitant from some far realm to a friend, describing the absurdities of mankind. It is true, as he said, that they would not do for publication, though certainly the manuscript contains some of his most delicious writing. Miss Wallace, to whom the next letter is written, had known Mark Twain in Bermuda, and, after his death, published a dainty volume entitled Mark Twain in the Happy Island.

"STORMFIELD," REDDING, CONNECTICUT,

Nov. 13, '09.

DEAR BETSY,—I've been writing "Letters from the Earth," and if you will come here and see us I will—what? Put the MS in your hands, with the places to skip marked? No. I won't trust you quite that far. I'll read messages to you. This book will never be published—in fact it couldn't be, because it would be felony to soil the mails with it, for it has much Holy Scripture in it of the kind that... can't properly be read aloud, except from the pulpit and in family worship. Paine enjoys it, but Paine is going to be damned one of these days, I suppose.

The autumn splendors passed you by? What a pity. I wish you had been here. It was beyond words! It was heaven and hell and sunset and rainbows and the aurora all fused into one divine harmony, and you couldn't look at it and keep the tears back. All the hosannahing strong gorgeousnesses have gone back to heaven and hell and the pole, now, but no matter; if you could look out of my bedroom window at this moment, you would choke up; and when you got your voice you would say: This is not real, this is a dream. Such a singing together, and such a whispering together, and such a snuggling together of cosy soft colors, and such kissing and caressing, and such pretty blushing when the sun breaks out and catches those dainty weeds at it—you remember that weed-garden of mine?—and then—then the far hills sleeping in a dim blue trance—oh, hearing about it is nothing, you should be here to see it.

Good! I wish I could go on the platform and read. And I could, if it could be kept out of the papers. There's a charity-school of 400 young girls in Boston that I would give my ears to talk to, if I had some more; but—oh, well, I can't go, and it's no use to grieve about it.

This morning Jean went to town; also Paine; also the butler; also Katy; also the laundress. The cook and the maid, and the boy and the roustabout and Jean's coachman are left—just enough to make it lonesome, because they are around yet never visible. However, the Harpers are sending Leigh up to play billiards; therefore I shall survive.

Affectionately,

S. L. CLEMENS.

Early in June that year, Clemens had developed unmistakable symptoms

of heart trouble of a very serious nature. It was angina pectoris, and while to all appearances he was as well as ever and usually felt so, he was periodically visited by severe attacks of acute "breast pains" which, as the months passed, increased in frequency and severity. He was alarmed and distressed—not on his own account, but because of his daughter Jean—a handsome girl, who had long been subject to epileptic seizures. In case of his death he feared that Jean would be without permanent anchorage, his other daughter, Clara—following her marriage to Ossip Gabrilowitsch in October—having taken up residence abroad.

This anxiety was soon ended. On the morning of December 24th, Jean Clemens was found dead in her apartment. She was not drowned in her bath, as was reported, but died from heart exhaustion, the result of her malady and the shock of cold water.

[Questionable diagnosis! D.W. M.D.]

The blow to her father was terrible, but heavy as it was, one may perhaps understand that her passing in that swift, painless way must have afforded him a measure of relief.

To Mrs. Gabrilowitsch, in Europe:

REDDING, CONN.,

Dec. 29, '09.

O, Clara, Clara dear, I am so glad she is out of it and safe—safe! I am not melancholy; I shall never be melancholy again, I think. You see, I was in such distress when I came to realize that you were gone far away and no one stood between her and danger but me—and I could die at any moment, and then—oh then what would become of her! For she was wilful, you know, and would not have been governable.

You can't imagine what a darling she was, that last two or three days; and how fine, and good, and sweet, and noble-and joyful, thank Heaven!—and how intellectually brilliant. I had never been acquainted with Jean before. I recognized that.

But I mustn't try to write about her—I can't. I have already poured my heart out with the pen, recording that last day or two.

I will send you that—and you must let no one but Ossip read it.

Good-bye.

I love you so!

And Ossip.

FATHER.

The writing mentioned in the last paragraph was his article 'The Death of Jean,' his last serious writing, and one of the world's most beautiful examples of elegiac prose.—[Harper's Magazine, Dec., 1910,] and later in the volume, 'What Is Man and Other Essays.'

XLVIII. LETTERS OF 1910. LAST TRIP TO BERMUDA. LETTERS TO PAINE. THE LAST LETTER.

Mark Twain had returned from a month's trip to Bermuda a few days before Jean died. Now, by his physician's advice, he went back to those balmy islands. He had always loved them, since his first trip there with Twichell thirty-three years earlier, and at "Bay House," the residence of Vice-Consul Allen, where he was always a welcome guest, he could have the attentions and care and comforts of a home. Taking Claude, the butler, as his valet, he sailed January 5th, and presently sent back a letter in which he said, "Again I am leading the ideal life, and am immeasurably content."

By his wish, the present writer and his family were keeping the Stormfield house open for him, in order that he might be able to return to its comforts at any time. He sent frequent letters—one or two by each steamer—but as a rule they did not concern matters of general interest. A little after his arrival, however, he wrote concerning an incident of his former visit—a trivial matter—but one which had annoyed him. I had been with him in Bermuda on the earlier visit, and as I remember it, there had been some slight oversight on his part in the matter of official etiquette—something which doubtless no one had noticed but himself.

To A. B. Paine, in Redding:

BAY HOUSE, Jan. 11, 1910.

DEAR PAINE,—... There was a military lecture last night at the Officer's Mess, prospect, and as the lecturer honored me with a special and urgent invitation and said he wanted to lecture to me particularly, I being "the greatest living master of the platform-art," I naturally packed Helen and her mother into the provided carriage and went.

As soon as we landed at the door with the crowd the Governor came to me at once and was very cordial, and apparently as glad to see me as he said he was. So that incident is closed. And pleasantly and entirely satisfactorily. Everything is all right, now, and I am no longer in a clumsy and awkward situation.

I "met up" with that charming Colonel Chapman, and other officers of the regiment, and had a good time.

Commandant Peters of the "Carnegie" will dine here tonight and arrange a private visit for us to his ship, the crowd to be denied access.

Sincerely Yours,

S. L. C.

"Helen" of this letter was Mr. and Mrs. Allen's young daughter, a favorite companion of his walks and drives. "Loomis" and "Lark," mentioned in the letters which follow, were Edward E. Loomis—his nephew by marriage—named by Mark Twain as one of the trustees of his estate, and Charles T. Lark, Mark Twain's attorney.

To A. B. Paine, in Redding:

HAMILTON, Jan. 21, '10.

DEAR PAINE,—Thanks for your letter, and for its contenting news of the situation in that foreign and far-off and vaguely-remembered country where you and Loomis and Lark and other beloved friends are.

I have a letter from Clara this morning. She is solicitous, and wants me well and watchfully taken care of. My, she ought to see Helen and her parents and Claude administer that trust!

Also she says: "I hope to hear from you or Mr. Paine very soon."

I am writing her, and I know you will respond to your part of her prayer. She is pretty desolate now, after Jean's emancipation—the only kindness God ever did that poor unoffending child in all her hard life.

Ys ever

S. L. C.

Send Clara a copy of Howells's gorgeous letter. I want a copy of my article that he is speaking of.

The "gorgeous letter" was concerning Mark Twain's article, "The Turning-point in My Life" which had just appeared in one of the Harper publications. Howells wrote of it, "While your wonderful words are warm in my mind yet, I want to tell you what you know already: that you never wrote anything greater, finer, than that turning-point paper of yours."

From the early Bermuda letters we may gather that Mark Twain's days were enjoyable enough, and that his malady was not giving him serious trouble, thus far. Near the end of January he wrote: "Life continues here the same as usual. There isn't a flaw in it. Good times, good home, tranquil contentment all day and every day, without a break. I shouldn't know how to go about bettering my situation." He did little in the way of literary work, probably finding neither time nor inclination for it. When he wrote at all it was merely to set down some fanciful drolleries with no thought of publication.

To Prof. William Lyon Phelps, Yale College:

HAMILTON, March 12.

DEAR PROFESSOR PHELPS,—I thank you ever so much for the book—[Professor Phelps's Essays on Modern Novelists.]—which I find charming—so charming indeed, that I read it through in a single night, and did not regret the lost night's sleep. I am glad if I deserve what you have said about me: and even if I don't I am proud and well contented, since you think I deserve it.

Yes, I saw Prof. Lounsbury, and had a most pleasant time with him. He ought to have staid longer in this little paradise—partly for his own sake, but mainly for mine.

I knew my poor Jean had written you. I shall not have so dear and sweet a secretary again.

Good health to you, and all good fortune attend you.

Sincerely yours,

S. L. CLEMENS.

He would appear to have written not many letters besides those to Mrs. Gabrilowitsch and to Stormfield, but when a little girl sent him a report of a dream, inspired by reading The Prince and the

Pauper, he took the time and trouble to acknowledge it, realizing, no doubt, that a line from him would give the child happiness.

To Miss Sulamith, in New York:

"BAY HOUSE," BERMUDA, March 21, 1910.

DEAR MISS SULAMITH,—I think it is a remarkable dream for a girl of 13 to have dreamed, in fact for a person of any age to have dreamed, because it moves by regular grade and sequence from the beginning to the end, which is not the habit of dreams. I think your report of it is a good piece of work, a clear and effective statement of the vision.

I am glad to know you like the "Prince and the Pauper" so well and I believe with you that the dream is good evidence of that liking. I think I may say, with your sister that I like myself best when I am serious.

Sincerely yours,

S. L. CLEMENS.

Through February, and most of March, letters and reports from him were about the same. He had begun to plan for his return, and concerning amusements at Stormfield for the entertainment of the neighbors, and for the benefit of the library which he had founded soon after his arrival in Redding. In these letters he seldom mentioned the angina pains that had tortured him earlier. But once, when he sent a small photograph of himself, it seemed to us that his face had become thin and that he had suffered. Certainly his next letter was not reassuring.

To A. B. Paine, in Redding:

DEAR PAINE,—We must look into the magic-lantern business. Maybe the modern lantern is too elaborate and troublesome for back-settlement use, but we can inquire. We must have some kind of a show at "Stormfield" to entertain the countryside with.

We are booked to sail in the "Bermudian" April 23rd, but don't tell anybody, I don't want it known. I may have to go sooner if the pain in my breast doesn't mend its ways pretty considerably. I don't want to die here for this is an unkind place for a person in that condition. I should have to lie in the undertaker's cellar until the ship would remove me and it is dark down there and unpleasant.

The Colliers will meet me on the pier and I may stay with them a week or two before going home. It all depends on the breast pain—I don't want to die there. I am growing more and more particular about the place.

With love,

S. L. C.

This letter had been written by the hand of his "secretary," Helen Allen: writing had become an effort to him. Yet we did not suspect how rapidly the end was approaching and only grew vaguely alarmed. A week later, however, it became evident that his condition was critical.

DEAR PAINE,—.... I have been having a most uncomfortable time for the past 4 days with that breast-pain, which turns out to be an affection of the heart, just as I originally suspected. The news from New York is to the effect that non-bronchial weather has arrived there at last, therefore if I can get my breast trouble in traveling condition I may sail for home a week or two earlier than has heretofore been proposed:

Yours as ever

S. L. CLEMENS,

(per H. S. A.)

In this letter he seems to have forgotten that his trouble had been pronounced an affection of the heart long before he left America, though at first it had been thought that it might be gastritis. The same mail brought a letter from Mr. Allen explaining fully the seriousness of his condition. I sailed immediately for Bermuda, arriving there on the 4th of April. He was not suffering at the moment, though the pains came now with alarming frequency and violence. He was cheerful and brave. He did not complain. He gave no suggestion of a man whose days were nearly ended.

A part of the Stormfield estate had been a farm, which he had given to Jean Clemens, where she had busied herself raising some live stock and poultry. After her death he had wished the place to be sold and the returns devoted to some memorial purpose. The sale had been made during the winter and the price received had been paid in cash. I found him full of interest in all affairs, and anxious to discuss the memorial plan. A day or two later he dictated the following letter-the last he would ever send.

It seemed fitting that this final word from one who had so long given happiness to the whole world should record a special gift to his neighbors.

To Charles T. Lark, in New York:

HAMILTON, BERMUDA.

April 6, 1910.

DEAR MR. LARK,—I have told Paine that I want the money derived from the sale of the farm, which I had given, but not conveyed, to my daughter Jean, to be used to erect a building for the Mark Twain Library of Redding, the building to be called the Jean L. Clemens Memorial Building.

I wish to place the money $6,000.00 in the hands of three trustees,—Paine and two others: H. A. Lounsbury and William E. Hazen, all of Redding, these trustees to form a building Committee to decide on the size and plan of the building needed and to arrange for and supervise the work in such a manner that the fund shall amply provide for the building complete, with necessary furnishings, leaving, if possible, a balance remaining, sufficient for such repairs and additional furnishings as may be required for two years from the time of completion.

Will you please draw a document covering these requirements and have it ready by the time I reach New York (April 14th).

Very sincerely,

S. L. CLEMENS.

We sailed on the 12th of April, reaching New York on the 14th, as he had planned. A day or two later, Mr. and Mrs. Gabrilowitsch, summoned from Italy by cable, arrived. He suffered very little after reaching Stormfield, and his mind was comparatively clear up to the last day. On the afternoon of April 21st he sank into a state of coma, and just at sunset he died. Three days later, at

Elmira, New York, he was laid beside Mrs. Clemens and those others who had preceded him.

THE LAST DAY AT STORMFIELD

By BLISS CARMAN.

At Redding, Connecticut,
The April sunrise pours
Over the hardwood ridges
Softening and greening now
In the first magic of Spring.

The wild cherry-trees are in bloom,
The bloodroot is white underfoot,
The serene early light flows on,

Touching with glory the world,
And flooding the large upper room
Where a sick man sleeps.
Slowly he opens his eyes,
After long weariness, smiles,
And stretches arms overhead,
While those about him take heart.

With his awakening strength,
(Morning and spring in the air,

The strong clean scents of earth,

The call of the golden shaft,

Ringing across the hills)

He takes up his heartening book,

Opens the volume and reads,

A page of old rugged Carlyle,

The dour philosopher

Who looked askance upon life,

Lurid, ironical, grim,

Yet sound at the core.

But weariness returns;

He lays the book aside

With his glasses upon the bed,

And gladly sleeps. Sleep,

Blessed abundant sleep,

Is all that he needs.

And when the close of day

Reddens upon the hills

And washes the room with rose,

In the twilight hush

The Summoner comes to him

Ever so gently, unseen,

Touches him on the shoulder;

And with the departing sun

Our great funning friend is gone.

How he has made us laugh!

A whole generation of men

Smiled in the joy of his wit.

But who knows whether he was not

Like those deep jesters of old

Who dwelt at the courts of Kings,

Arthur's, Pendragon's, Lear's,

Plying the wise fool's trade,

Making men merry at will,

Hiding their deeper thoughts

Under a motley array,—

Keen-eyed, serious men,

Watching the sorry world,

The gaudy pageant of life,

With pity and wisdom and love?

Fearless, extravagant, wild,

His caustic merciless mirth

Was leveled at pompous shams.

Doubt not behind that mask

There dwelt the soul of a man,

Resolute, sorrowing, sage,

As sure a champion of good

As ever rode forth to fray.

Haply—who knows?—somewhere

In Avalon, Isle of Dreams,

In vast contentment at last,

With every grief done away,

While Chaucer and Shakespeare wait,

And Moliere hangs on his words,

And Cervantes not far off

Listens and smiles apart,

With that incomparable drawl

He is jesting with Dagonet now.

About Author

Samuel Langhorne Clemens (November 30, 1835 – April 21, 1910), known by his pen name Mark Twain, was an American writer, humorist, entrepreneur, publisher, and lecturer. He was lauded as the "greatest humorist this country has produced", and William Faulkner called him "the father of American literature". His novels include The Adventures of Tom Sawyer (1876) and its sequel, the Adventures of Huckleberry Finn (1884), the latter often called "The Great American Novel".

Twain was raised in Hannibal, Missouri, which later provided the setting for Tom Sawyer and Huckleberry Finn. He served an apprenticeship with a printer and then worked as a typesetter, contributing articles to the newspaper of his older brother Orion Clemens. He later became a riverboat pilot on the Mississippi River before heading west to join Orion in Nevada. He referred humorously to his lack of success at mining, turning to journalism for the Virginia City Territorial Enterprise. His humorous story, "The Celebrated Jumping Frog of Calaveras County", was published in 1865, based on a story that he heard at Angels Hotel in Angels Camp, California, where he had spent some time as a miner. The short story brought international attention and was even translated into French. His wit and satire, in prose and in speech, earned praise from critics and peers, and he was a friend to presidents, artists, industrialists, and European royalty.

Twain earned a great deal of money from his writings and lectures, but he invested in ventures that lost most of it—such as the Paige Compositor, a mechanical typesetter that failed because of its complexity and imprecision. He filed for bankruptcy in the wake of these financial setbacks, but he eventually overcame his financial troubles with the help of Henry Huttleston Rogers. He eventually paid all his creditors in full, even though his bankruptcy relieved him of having to do so.

Twain was born shortly after an appearance of Halley's Comet, and he predicted that he would "go out with it" as well; he died the day after the comet returned.

Biography

Early life

Samuel Langhorne Clemens was born on November 30, 1835, in Florida, Missouri, the sixth of seven children born to Jane (née Lampton; 1803–1890), a native of Kentucky, and John Marshall Clemens (1798–1847), a native of Virginia. His parents met when his father moved to Missouri, and they were married in 1823. Twain was of Cornish, English, and Scots-Irish descent. Only three of his siblings survived childhood: Orion (1825–1897), Henry (1838–1858), and Pamela (1827–1904). His sister Margaret (1830–1839) died when Twain was three, and his brother Benjamin (1832–1842) died three years later. His brother Pleasant Hannibal (1828) died at three weeks of age.

When he was four, Twain's family moved to Hannibal, Missouri, a port town on the Mississippi River that inspired the fictional town of St. Petersburg in The Adventures of Tom Sawyer and the Adventures of Huckleberry Finn. Slavery was legal in Missouri at the time, and it became a theme in these writings. His father was an attorney and judge, who died of pneumonia in 1847, when Twain was 11. The next year, Twain left school after the fifth grade to become a printer's apprentice. In 1851, he began working as a typesetter, contributing articles and humorous sketches to the Hannibal Journal, a newspaper that Orion owned. When he was 18, he left Hannibal and worked as a printer in New York City, Philadelphia, St. Louis, and Cincinnati, joining the newly formed International Typographical Union, the printers trade union. He educated himself in public libraries in the evenings, finding wider information than at a conventional school.

Twain describes his boyhood in Life on the Mississippi, stating that "there was but one permanent ambition" among his comrades: to be a steamboatman.

Pilot was the grandest position of all. The pilot, even in those days of trivial wages, had a princely salary – from a hundred and fifty to two hundred and fifty dollars a month, and no board to pay.

As Twain describes it, the pilot's prestige exceeded that of the captain. The pilot had to:

> ...get up a warm personal acquaintanceship with every old snag and one-limbed cottonwood and every obscure wood pile that ornaments the banks of this river for twelve hundred miles; and more than that, must... actually know where these things are in the dark

Steamboat pilot Horace E. Bixby took Twain on as a cub pilot to teach him the river between New Orleans and St. Louis for $500 (equivalent to $14,000 in 2018), payable out of Twain's first wages after graduating. Twain studied the Mississippi, learning its landmarks, how to navigate its currents effectively, and how to read the river and its constantly shifting channels, reefs, submerged snags, and rocks that would "tear the life out of the strongest vessel that ever floated". It was more than two years before he received his pilot's license. Piloting also gave him his pen name from "mark twain", the leadsman's cry for a measured river depth of two fathoms (12 feet), which was safe water for a steamboat.

As a young pilot, Clemens served on the steamer A. B. Chambers with Grant Marsh, who became famous for his exploits as a steamboat captain on the Missouri River. The two liked each other, and admired one another, and maintained a correspondence for many years after Clemens left the river.

While training, Samuel convinced his younger brother Henry to work with him, and even arranged a post of mud clerk for him on the steamboat Pennsylvania. On June 13, 1858, the steamboat's boiler exploded; Henry succumbed to his wounds on June 21. Twain claimed to have foreseen this death in a dream a month earlier, which inspired his interest in parapsychology; he was an early member of the Society for Psychical Research. Twain was guilt-stricken and held himself responsible for the rest of his life. He continued to work on the river and was a river pilot until the Civil War broke out in 1861, when traffic was curtailed along the Mississippi River. At the start of hostilities, he enlisted briefly in a local Confederate unit. He later wrote the sketch "The Private History of a Campaign That Failed", describing how he and his friends had been Confederate volunteers for two weeks before disbanding.

He then left for Nevada to work for his brother Orion, who was Secretary of the Nevada Territory. Twain describes the episode in his book Roughing It.

Travels

Orion became secretary to Nevada Territory governor James W. Nye in 1861, and Twain joined him when he moved west. The brothers traveled more than two weeks on a stagecoach across the Great Plains and the Rocky Mountains, visiting the Mormon community in Salt Lake City.

Twain's journey ended in the silver-mining town of Virginia City, Nevada, where he became a miner on the Comstock Lode. He failed as a miner and went to work at the Virginia City newspaper Territorial Enterprise, working under a friend, the writer Dan DeQuille. He first used his pen name here on February 3, 1863, when he wrote a humorous travel account entitled "Letter From Carson – re: Joe Goodman; party at Gov. Johnson's; music" and signed it "Mark Twain".

His experiences in the American West inspired Roughing It, written during 1870–71 and published in 1872. His experiences in Angels Camp (in Calaveras County, California) provided material for "The Celebrated Jumping Frog of Calaveras County" (1865).

Twain moved to San Francisco in 1864, still as a journalist, and met writers such as Bret Harte and Artemus Ward. He may have been romantically involved with the poet Ina Coolbrith.

His first success as a writer came when his humorous tall tale "The Celebrated Jumping Frog of Calaveras County" was published on November 18, 1865, in the New York weekly The Saturday Press, bringing him national attention. A year later, he traveled to the Sandwich Islands (present-day Hawaii) as a reporter for the Sacramento Union. His letters to the Union were popular and became the basis for his first lectures.

In 1867, a local newspaper funded his trip to the Mediterranean aboard the Quaker City, including a tour of Europe and the Middle East. He wrote a collection of travel letters which were later compiled as The Innocents Abroad (1869). It was on this trip that he met fellow passenger Charles Langdon, who showed him a picture of his sister Olivia. Twain later claimed to have fallen in love at first sight.

Upon returning to the United States, Twain was offered honorary membership in Yale University's secret society Scroll and Key in 1868. Its devotion to "fellowship, moral and literary self-improvement, and charity" suited him well.

Marriage and children

Twain and Olivia Langdon corresponded throughout 1868. She rejected his first marriage proposal, but they were married in Elmira, New York in February 1870, where he courted her and managed to overcome her father's initial reluctance. She came from a "wealthy but liberal family"; through her, he met abolitionists, "socialists, principled atheists and activists for women's rights and social equality", including Harriet Beecher Stowe (his next-door neighbor in Hartford, Connecticut), Frederick Douglass, and writer and utopian socialist William Dean Howells, who became a long-time friend. The couple lived in Buffalo, New York, from 1869 to 1871. He owned a stake in the Buffalo Express newspaper and worked as an editor and writer. While they were living in Buffalo, their son Langdon died of diphtheria at the age of 19 months. They had three daughters: Susy (1872–1896), Clara (1874–1962), and Jean (1880–1909).

Twain moved his family to Hartford, Connecticut, where he arranged the building of a home starting in 1873. In the 1870s and 1880s, the family summered at Quarry Farm in Elmira, the home of Olivia's sister, Susan Crane. In 1874, Susan had a study built apart from the main house so that Twain would have a quiet place in which to write. Also, he smoked cigars constantly, and Susan did not want him to do so in her house.

Twain wrote many of his classic novels during his 17 years in Hartford (1874–1891) and over 20 summers at Quarry Farm. They include The Adventures of Tom Sawyer (1876), The Prince and the Pauper (1881), Life on the Mississippi (1883), Adventures of Huckleberry Finn (1884), and A

Connecticut Yankee in King Arthur's Court (1889).

The couple's marriage lasted 34 years until Olivia's death in 1904. All of the Clemens family are buried in Elmira's Woodlawn Cemetery.

Love of science and technology

Twain was fascinated with science and scientific inquiry. He developed a close and lasting friendship with Nikola Tesla, and the two spent much time together in Tesla's laboratory.

Twain patented three inventions, including an "Improvement in Adjustable and Detachable Straps for Garments" (to replace suspenders) and a history trivia game. Most commercially successful was a self-pasting scrapbook; a dried adhesive on the pages needed only to be moistened before use. Over 25,000 were sold.

Twain was an early proponent of fingerprinting as a forensic technique, featuring it in a tall tale in Life on the Mississippi (1883) and as a central plot element in the novel Pudd'nhead Wilson (1894).

Twain's novel A Connecticut Yankee in King Arthur's Court (1889) features a time traveler from the contemporary U.S., using his knowledge of science to introduce modern technology to Arthurian England. This type of historical manipulation became a trope of speculative fiction as alternate histories.

In 1909, Thomas Edison visited Twain at his home in Redding, Connecticut and filmed him. Part of the footage was used in The Prince and the Pauper (1909), a two-reel short film. It is the only known existing film footage of Twain.

Financial troubles

Twain made a substantial amount of money through his writing, but he lost a great deal through investments. He invested mostly in new inventions and technology, particularly the Paige typesetting machine. It was a beautifully engineered mechanical marvel that amazed viewers when it worked, but it was prone to breakdowns. Twain spent $300,000 (equal to $9,000,000 in inflation-adjusted terms) on it between 1880 and 1894, but before it could be perfected it was rendered obsolete by the Linotype. He lost the bulk of his book profits, as well as a substantial portion of his wife's inheritance.

Twain also lost money through his publishing house, Charles L. Webster and Company, which enjoyed initial success selling the memoirs of Ulysses S. Grant but failed soon afterward, losing money on a biography of Pope Leo XIII. Fewer than 200 copies were sold.

Twain and his family closed down their expensive Hartford home in response to the dwindling income and moved to Europe in June 1891. William M. Laffan of The New York Sun and the McClure Newspaper Syndicate offered him the publication of a series of six European letters. Twain, Olivia, and their daughter Susy were all faced with health problems, and they believed that it would be of benefit to visit European baths. The family stayed mainly in France, Germany, and Italy until May 1895, with longer spells at Berlin (winter 1891/92), Florence (fall and winter 1892/93), and Paris (winters and springs 1893/94 and 1894/95). During that period, Twain returned four times to New York due to his enduring business troubles. He took "a cheap room" in September 1893 at $1.50 per day (equivalent to $42 in 2018) at The Players Club, which he had to keep until March 1894; meanwhile, he became "the Belle of New York," in the words of biographer Albert Bigelow Paine.

Twain's writings and lectures enabled him to recover financially, combined with the help of his friend, Henry Huttleston Rogers. He began a friendship with the financier in 1893, a principal of Standard Oil, that lasted the remainder of his life. Rogers first made him file for bankruptcy in April 1894, then had him transfer the copyrights on his written works to his wife to prevent creditors from gaining possession of them. Finally, Rogers took absolute charge of Twain's money until all his creditors were paid.

Twain accepted an offer from Robert Sparrow Smythe and embarked on a year-long, around the world lecture tour in July 1895 to pay off his creditors in full, although he was no longer under any legal obligation to do so. It was a long, arduous journey and he was sick much of the time, mostly from a cold and a carbuncle. The first part of the itinerary took him across northern America to British Columbia, Canada, until the second half of August. For the second part, he sailed across the Pacific Ocean. His scheduled lecture in Honolulu, Hawaii had to be canceled due to a cholera epidemic. Twain went on to Fiji, Australia, New Zealand, Sri Lanka, India, Mauritius, and South Africa. His three months in India became the centerpiece of his 712-page book Following the Equator. In the second half of July 1896, he sailed back to England, completing his circumnavigation of the world begun 14 months before.

Twain and his family spent four more years in Europe, mainly in England and Austria (October 1897 to May 1899), with longer spells in London and Vienna. Clara had wished to study the piano under Theodor Leschetizky in Vienna. However, Jean's health did not benefit from consulting with specialists in Vienna, the "City of Doctors". The family moved to London in spring 1899, following a lead by Poultney Bigelow who had a good experience being treated by Dr. Jonas Henrik Kellgren, a Swedish osteopathic practitioner in Belgravia. They were persuaded to spend the summer at Kellgren's sanatorium by the lake in the Swedish village of Sanna. Coming back in fall, they continued the treatment in London, until Twain was convinced by lengthy inquiries in America that similar osteopathic expertise was available there.

In mid-1900, he was the guest of newspaper proprietor Hugh Gilzean-Reid at Dollis Hill House, located on the north side of London. Twain wrote that he had "never seen any place that was so satisfactorily situated, with its noble trees and stretch of country, and everything that went to make life delightful, and all within a biscuit's throw of the metropolis of the world." He then returned to America in October 1900, having earned enough to pay off his debts. In winter 1900/01, he became his country's most prominent opponent of imperialism, raising the issue in his speeches, interviews, and writings. In January 1901, he began serving as vice-president of the Anti-Imperialist League of New York.

Speaking engagements

Twain was in great demand as a featured speaker, performing solo humorous talks similar to modern stand-up comedy. He gave paid talks to many men's clubs, including the Authors' Club, Beefsteak Club, Vagabonds, White Friars, and Monday Evening Club of Hartford.

In the late 1890s, he spoke to the Savage Club in London and was elected an honorary member. He was told that only three men had been so honored, including the Prince of Wales, and he replied: "Well, it must make the Prince feel mighty fine." He visited Melbourne and Sydney in 1895 as part of a world lecture tour. In 1897, he spoke to the Concordia Press Club in Vienna as a special guest, following the diplomat Charlemagne Tower, Jr. He delivered the speech "Die Schrecken der Deutschen Sprache" ("The Horrors of the German Language")—in German—to the great amusement of the audience. In 1901, he was invited to speak at Princeton University's Cliosophic Literary Society, where he was made an honorary member.

Canadian visits

In 1881, Twain was honored at a banquet in Montreal, Canada where he made reference to securing a copyright. In 1883, he paid a brief visit to Ottawa, and he visited Toronto twice in 1884 and 1885 on a reading tour with George Washington Cable, known as the "Twins of Genius" tour.

The reason for the Toronto visits was to secure Canadian and British copyrights for his upcoming book Adventures of Huckleberry Finn, to which he had alluded in his Montreal visit. The reason for the Ottawa visit had been to secure Canadian and British copyrights for Life on the Mississippi. Publishers in Toronto had printed unauthorized editions of his books at the time, before an international copyright agreement was established in 1891. These were sold in the United States as well as in Canada, depriving him of royalties. He estimated that Belford Brothers' edition of The Adventures of Tom Sawyer alone had cost him ten thousand dollars (equivalent to $280,000 in 2018). He had unsuccessfully attempted to secure the rights for The Prince and the Pauper in 1881, in conjunction with his Montreal trip. Eventually, he received legal advice to register a copyright in Canada (for both Canada and Britain) prior to publishing in the United States, which would restrain the Canadian publishers from printing a version when the American edition was published. There was a requirement that a copyright be registered to a Canadian resident; he addressed this by his short visits to the country.

Later life and death

... the report is greatly exaggerated.

—Twain's reaction to a report of his death

Twain lived in his later years at 14 West 10th Street in Manhattan. He passed through a period of deep depression which began in 1896 when his daughter Susy died of meningitis. Olivia's death in 1904 and Jean's on December 24, 1909, deepened his gloom. On May 20, 1909, his close friend Henry Rogers died suddenly. In 1906, Twain began his autobiography in the North American Review. In April, he heard that his friend Ina Coolbrith had lost nearly all that she owned in the 1906 San Francisco earthquake, and he volunteered a few autographed portrait photographs to be sold for her benefit. To further aid Coolbrith, George Wharton James visited Twain in New York and arranged for a new portrait session. He was resistant initially, but he eventually admitted that four of the resulting images were the finest ones ever taken of him.

Twain formed a club in 1906 for girls whom he viewed as surrogate granddaughters called the Angel Fish and Aquarium Club. The dozen or so members ranged in age from 10 to 16. He exchanged letters with his "Angel Fish" girls and invited them to concerts and the theatre and to play games. Twain wrote in 1908 that the club was his "life's chief delight". In 1907, he met Dorothy Quick (aged 11) on a transatlantic crossing, beginning "a friendship that was to last until the very day of his death".

Oxford University awarded Twain an honorary doctorate in letters in 1907.

Twain was born two weeks after Halley's Comet's closest approach in 1835; he said in 1909:

I came in with Halley's Comet in 1835. It is coming again next year, and I expect to go out with it. It will be the greatest disappointment of my life if

I don't go out with Halley's Comet. The Almighty has said, no doubt: "Now here are these two unaccountable freaks; they came in together, they must go out together".

Twain's prediction was accurate; he died of a heart attack on April 21, 1910, in Redding, Connecticut, one day after the comet's closest approach to Earth.

Upon hearing of Twain's death, President William Howard Taft said:

Mark Twain gave pleasure – real intellectual enjoyment – to millions, and his works will continue to give such pleasure to millions yet to come … His humor was American, but he was nearly as much appreciated by Englishmen and people of other countries as by his own countrymen. He has made an enduring part of American literature.

Twain's funeral was at the Brick Presbyterian Church on Fifth Avenue, New York. He is buried in his wife's family plot at Woodlawn Cemetery in Elmira, New York. The Langdon family plot is marked by a 12-foot monument (two fathoms, or "mark twain") placed there by his surviving daughter Clara. There is also a smaller headstone. He expressed a preference for cremation (for example, in Life on the Mississippi), but he acknowledged that his surviving family would have the last word.

Officials in Connecticut and New York estimated the value of Twain's estate at $471,000 ($13,000,000 today).

Writing

Overview

Twain began his career writing light, humorous verse, but he became a chronicler of the vanities, hypocrisies, and murderous acts of mankind. At mid-career, he combined rich humor, sturdy narrative, and social criticism in Huckleberry Finn. He was a master of rendering colloquial speech and helped to create and popularize a distinctive American literature built on American themes and language.

Many of his works have been suppressed at times for various reasons. The

Adventures of Huckleberry Finn has been repeatedly restricted in American high schools, not least for its frequent use of the word "nigger", which was in common usage in the pre-Civil War period in which the novel was set.

A complete bibliography of Twain's works is nearly impossible to compile because of the vast number of pieces he wrote (often in obscure newspapers) and his use of several different pen names. Additionally, a large portion of his speeches and lectures have been lost or were not recorded; thus, the compilation of Twain's works is an ongoing process. Researchers rediscovered published material as recently as 1995 and 2015.

Early journalism and travelogues

Twain was writing for the Virginia City newspaper the Territorial Enterprise in 1863 when he met lawyer Tom Fitch, editor of the competing newspaper Virginia Daily Union and known as the "silver-tongued orator of the Pacific". He credited Fitch with giving him his "first really profitable lesson" in writing. "When I first began to lecture, and in my earlier writings," Twain later commented, "my sole idea was to make comic capital out of everything I saw and heard." In 1866, he presented his lecture on the Sandwich Islands to a crowd in Washoe City, Nevada. Afterwards, Fitch told him:

Clemens, your lecture was magnificent. It was eloquent, moving, sincere. Never in my entire life have I listened to such a magnificent piece of descriptive narration. But you committed one unpardonable sin – the unpardonable sin. It is a sin you must never commit again. You closed a most eloquent description, by which you had keyed your audience up to a pitch of the intensest interest, with a piece of atrocious anti-climax which nullified all the really fine effect you had produced.

It was in these days that Twain became a writer of the Sagebrush School; he was known later as its most famous member. His first important work was "The Celebrated Jumping Frog of Calaveras County," published in the New York Saturday Press on November 18, 1865. After a burst of popularity, the Sacramento Union commissioned him to write letters about his travel experiences. The first journey that he took for this job was to ride the steamer Ajax on its maiden voyage to the Sandwich Islands (Hawaii).

All the while, he was writing letters to the newspaper that were meant for publishing, chronicling his experiences with humor. These letters proved to be the genesis to his work with the San Francisco Alta California newspaper, which designated him a traveling correspondent for a trip from San Francisco to New York City via the Panama isthmus.

On June 8, 1867, he set sail on the pleasure cruiser Quaker City for five months, and this trip resulted in The Innocents Abroad or The New Pilgrims' Progress. In 1872, he published his second piece of travel literature, Roughing It, as an account of his journey from Missouri to Nevada, his subsequent life in the American West, and his visit to Hawaii. The book lampoons American and Western society in the same way that Innocents critiqued the various countries of Europe and the Middle East. His next work was The Gilded Age: A Tale of Today, his first attempt at writing a novel. The book, written with his neighbor Charles Dudley Warner, is also his only collaboration.

Twain's next work drew on his experiences on the Mississippi River. Old Times on the Mississippi was a series of sketches published in the Atlantic Monthly in 1875 featuring his disillusionment with Romanticism. Old Times eventually became the starting point for Life on the Mississippi.

Tom Sawyer and Huckleberry Finn

Twain's next major publication was The Adventures of Tom Sawyer, which draws on his youth in Hannibal. Tom Sawyer was modeled on Twain as a child, with traces of schoolmates John Briggs and Will Bowen. The book also introduces Huckleberry Finn in a supporting role, based on Twain's boyhood friend Tom Blankenship.

The Prince and the Pauper was not as well received, despite a storyline that is common in film and literature today. The book tells the story of two boys born on the same day who are physically identical, acting as a social commentary as the prince and pauper switch places. Twain had started Adventures of Huckleberry Finn (which he consistently had problems completing) and had completed his travel book A Tramp Abroad, which describes his travels through central and southern Europe.

Twain's next major published work was the Adventures of Huckleberry Finn, which confirmed him as a noteworthy American writer. Some have called it the first Great American Novel, and the book has become required reading in many schools throughout the United States. Huckleberry Finn was an offshoot from Tom Sawyer and had a more serious tone than its predecessor. Four hundred manuscript pages were written in mid-1876, right after the publication of Tom Sawyer. The last fifth of Huckleberry Finn is subject to much controversy. Some say that Twain experienced a "failure of nerve," as critic Leo Marx puts it. Ernest Hemingway once said of Huckleberry Finn:

If you read it, you must stop where the Nigger Jim is stolen from the boys. That is the real end. The rest is just cheating.

Hemingway also wrote in the same essay:

All modern American literature comes from one book by Mark Twain called Huckleberry Finn.

Near the completion of Huckleberry Finn, Twain wrote Life on the Mississippi, which is said to have heavily influenced the novel. The travel work recounts Twain's memories and new experiences after a 22-year absence from the Mississippi River. In it, he also explains that "Mark Twain" was the call made when the boat was in safe water, indicating a depth of two fathoms (12 feet or 3.7 metres).

Later writing

Twain produced President Ulysses S. Grant's Memoirs through his fledgling publishing house, Charles L. Webster & Company, which he co-owned with Charles L. Webster, his nephew by marriage.

At this time he also wrote "The Private History of a Campaign That Failed" for The Century Magazine. This piece detailed his two-week stint in a Confederate militia during the Civil War. He next focused on A Connecticut Yankee in King Arthur's Court, written with the same historical fiction style as The Prince and the Pauper. A Connecticut Yankee showed the absurdities of political and social norms by setting them in the court of King Arthur. The book was started in December 1885, then shelved a few months later until the summer of 1887, and eventually finished in the spring of 1889.

His next large-scale work was Pudd'nhead Wilson, which he wrote rapidly, as he was desperately trying to stave off bankruptcy. From November 12 to December 14, 1893, Twain wrote 60,000 words for the novel. Critics[who?] have pointed to this rushed completion as the cause of the novel's rough organization and constant disruption of the plot. This novel also contains the tale of two boys born on the same day who switch positions in life, like The Prince and the Pauper. It was first published serially in Century Magazine and, when it was finally published in book form, Pudd'nhead Wilson appeared as the main title; however, the "subtitles" make the entire title read: The Tragedy of Pudd'nhead Wilson and the Comedy of The Extraordinary Twins.

Twain's next venture was a work of straight fiction that he called Personal Recollections of Joan of Arc and dedicated to his wife. He had long said[where?] that this was the work that he was most proud of, despite the criticism that he received for it. The book had been a dream of his since childhood, and he claimed that he had found a manuscript detailing the life of Joan of Arc when he was an adolescent. This was another piece that he was convinced would save his publishing company. His financial adviser Henry Huttleston Rogers quashed that idea and got Twain out of that business altogether, but the book was published nonetheless.[citation needed]

To pay the bills and keep his business projects afloat, Twain had begun to write articles and commentary furiously, with diminishing returns, but it was not enough. He filed for bankruptcy in 1894. During this time of dire financial straits, he published several literary reviews in newspapers to help make ends meet. He famously derided James Fenimore Cooper in his article detailing Cooper's "Literary Offenses". He became an extremely outspoken critic of other authors and other critics; he suggested that, before praising Cooper's work, Thomas Lounsbury, Brander Matthews, and Wilkie Collins "ought to have read some of it".

George Eliot, Jane Austen, and Robert Louis Stevenson also fell under Twain's attack during this time period, beginning around 1890 and continuing until his death. He outlines what he considers to be "quality writing" in several letters and essays, in addition to providing a source for the "tooth and claw" style of literary criticism. He places emphasis on concision, utility of word choice, and realism; he complains, for example, that Cooper's Deerslayer purports to be realistic but has several shortcomings. Ironically, several of his own works were later criticized for lack of continuity (Adventures of Huckleberry Finn) and organization (Pudd'nhead Wilson).

Twain's wife died in 1904 while the couple were staying at the Villa di Quarto in Florence. After some time had passed he published some works that his wife, his de facto editor and censor throughout her married life, had looked down upon. The Mysterious Stranger is perhaps the best known, depicting various visits of Satan to earth. This particular work was not published in Twain's lifetime. His manuscripts included three versions, written between 1897 and 1905: the so-called Hannibal, Eseldorf, and Print Shop versions. The resulting confusion led to extensive publication of a jumbled version, and only recently have the original versions become available as Twain wrote them.

Twain's last work was his autobiography, which he dictated and thought would be most entertaining if he went off on whims and tangents in non-chronological order. Some archivists and compilers have rearranged the biography into a more conventional form, thereby eliminating some of Twain's humor and the flow of the book. The first volume of the autobiography, over 736 pages, was published by the University of California in November 2010, 100 years after his death, as Twain wished. It soon became an unexpected best-seller, making Twain one of a very few authors publishing new best-selling volumes in the 19th, 20th, and 21st centuries.

Censorship

Twain's works have been subjected to censorship efforts. According to Stuart (2013), "Leading these banning campaigns, generally, were religious organizations or individuals in positions of influence – not so much working librarians, who had been instilled with that American "library spirit" which honored intellectual freedom (within bounds of course)". In 1905, the Brooklyn Public Library banned both The Adventures of Huckleberry Finn and The Adventures of Tom Sawyer from the children's department because of their language.

Views

Twain's views became more radical as he grew older. In a letter to friend and fellow writer William Dean Howells in 1887 he acknowledged that his views had changed and developed over his lifetime, referring to one of his favorite works:

When I finished Carlyle's French Revolution in 1871, I was a Girondin; every time I have read it since, I have read it differently – being influenced and changed, little by little, by life and environment ... and now I lay the book down once more, and recognize that I am a Sansculotte! And not a pale, characterless Sansculotte, but a Marat.

Anti-imperialist

Before 1899, Twain was an ardent imperialist. In the late 1860s and early 1870s, he spoke out strongly in favor of American interests in the Hawaiian Islands. He said the war with Spain in 1898 was "the worthiest" war ever fought. In 1899, however, he reversed course. In the New York Herald, October 16, 1900, Twain describes his transformation and political awakening, in the context of the Philippine–American War, to anti-imperialism:

I wanted the American eagle to go screaming into the Pacific ... Why not spread its wings over the Philippines, I asked myself? ... I said to myself, Here are a people who have suffered for three centuries. We can make them as free as ourselves, give them a government and country of their own, put a miniature of the American Constitution afloat in the Pacific, start a brand new republic to take its place among the free nations of the world. It seemed to me a great task to which we had addressed ourselves.

But I have thought some more, since then, and I have read carefully the treaty of Paris [which ended the Spanish–American War], and I have seen that we do not intend to free, but to subjugate the people of the Philippines. We have gone there to conquer, not to redeem.

It should, it seems to me, be our pleasure and duty to make those people free, and let them deal with their own domestic questions in their own way. And so I am an anti-imperialist. I am opposed to having the eagle put its talons on any other land.

During the Boxer rebellion, Twain said that "the Boxer is a patriot. He loves his country better than he does the countries of other people. I wish him success."

From 1901, soon after his return from Europe, until his death in 1910, Twain was vice-president of the American Anti-Imperialist League, which opposed the annexation of the Philippines by the United States and had "tens of thousands of members". He wrote many political pamphlets for the organization. The Incident in the Philippines, posthumously published in 1924, was in response to the Moro Crater Massacre, in which six hundred Moros were killed. Many of his neglected and previously uncollected writings on anti-imperialism appeared for the first time in book form in 1992.

Twain was critical of imperialism in other countries as well. In Following the Equator, Twain expresses "hatred and condemnation of imperialism of all stripes". He was highly critical of European imperialists, such as Cecil Rhodes, who greatly expanded the British Empire, and Leopold II, King of the Belgians. King Leopold's Soliloquy is a stinging political satire about his private colony, the Congo Free State. Reports of outrageous exploitation and grotesque abuses led to widespread international protest in the early 1900s, arguably the first large-scale human rights movement. In the soliloquy, the King argues that bringing Christianity to the country outweighs a little starvation. Leopold's rubber gatherers were tortured, maimed and slaughtered until the movement forced Brussels to call a halt.

During the Philippine–American War, Twain wrote a short pacifist story titled The War Prayer, which makes the point that humanism and Christianity's preaching of love are incompatible with the conduct of war. It was submitted to Harper's Bazaar for publication, but on March 22, 1905, the magazine rejected the story as "not quite suited to a woman's magazine". Eight days later, Twain wrote to his friend Daniel Carter Beard, to whom he had read the story, "I don't think the prayer will be published in my time. None but the dead are permitted to tell the truth." Because he had an exclusive contract with Harper & Brothers, Twain could not publish The War Prayer elsewhere; it remained unpublished until 1923. It was republished as campaigning material by Vietnam War protesters.

Twain acknowledged that he had originally sympathized with the more moderate Girondins of the French Revolution and then shifted his sympathies to the more radical Sansculottes, indeed identifying himself as "a Marat" and writing that the Reign of Terror paled in comparison to the older terrors that preceded it. Twain supported the revolutionaries in Russia against the reformists, arguing that the Tsar must be got rid of by violent means, because peaceful ones would not work. He summed up his views of revolutions in the following statement:

I am said to be a revolutionist in my sympathies, by birth, by breeding and by principle. I am always on the side of the revolutionists, because there never was a revolution unless there were some oppressive and intolerable conditions against which to revolute.

Civil rights

Twain was an adamant supporter of the abolition of slavery and the emancipation of slaves, even going so far as to say, "Lincoln's Proclamation ... not only set the black slaves free, but set the white man free also". He argued that non-whites did not receive justice in the United States, once saying, "I have seen Chinamen abused and maltreated in all the mean, cowardly ways possible to the invention of a degraded nature ... but I never saw a Chinaman righted in a court of justice for wrongs thus done to him". He paid for at least one black person to attend Yale Law School and for another black person to attend a southern university to become a minister.

Twain's sympathetic views on race were not reflected in his early writings on American Indians. Of them, Twain wrote in 1870:

His heart is a cesspool of falsehood, of treachery, and of low and devilish instincts. With him, gratitude is an unknown emotion; and when one does him a kindness, it is safest to keep the face toward him, lest the reward be an arrow in the back. To accept of a favor from him is to assume a debt which you can never repay to his satisfaction, though you bankrupt yourself trying. The scum of the earth!

As counterpoint, Twain's essay on "The Literary Offenses of Fenimore Cooper" offers a much kinder view of Indians. "No, other Indians would have noticed these things, but Cooper's Indians never notice anything. Cooper thinks they are marvelous creatures for noticing, but he was almost always in error about his Indians. There was seldom a sane one among them." In his later travelogue Following the Equator (1897), Twain observes that in colonized lands all over the world, "savages" have always been wronged by "whites" in the most merciless ways, such as "robbery, humiliation, and slow, slow murder, through poverty and the white man's whiskey"; his conclusion is that "there are many humorous things in this world; among them the white man's notion that he is less savage than the other savages". In an expression that captures his East Indian experiences, he wrote, "So far as I am able to judge nothing has been left undone, either by man or Nature, to make India the most extraordinary country that the sun visits on his rounds. Where every prospect pleases, and only man is vile."

Twain was also a staunch supporter of women's rights and an active campaigner for women's suffrage. His "Votes for Women" speech, in which he pressed for the granting of voting rights to women, is considered one of the most famous in history.

Helen Keller benefited from Twain's support as she pursued her college education and publishing despite her disabilities and financial limitations. The two were friends for roughly 16 years.

Through Twain's efforts, the Connecticut legislature voted a pension for Prudence Crandall, since 1995 Connecticut's official heroine, for her efforts towards the education of African-American young ladies in Connecticut. Twain also offered to purchase for her use her former house in Canterbury, home of the Canterbury Female Boarding School, but she declined.

Labor

Twain wrote glowingly about unions in the river boating industry in Life on the Mississippi, which was read in union halls decades later. He supported the labor movement, especially one of the most important unions, the Knights of Labor. In a speech to them, he said:

Who are the oppressors? The few: the King, the capitalist, and a handful of other overseers and superintendents. Who are the oppressed? The many: the nations of the earth; the valuable personages; the workers; they that make the bread that the soft-handed and idle eat.

Religion

Twain was a Presbyterian. He was critical of organized religion and certain elements of Christianity through his later life. He wrote, for example, "Faith is believing what you know ain't so", and "If Christ were here now there is one thing he would not be – a Christian". With anti-Catholic sentiment rampant in 19th century America, Twain noted he was "educated to enmity toward everything that is Catholic". As an adult, he engaged in religious discussions and attended services, his theology developing as he wrestled with the deaths of loved ones and with his own mortality.

Twain generally avoided publishing his most controversial opinions on religion in his lifetime, and they are known from essays and stories that were published later. In the essay Three Statements of the Eighties in the 1880s, Twain stated that he believed in an almighty God, but not in any messages, revelations, holy scriptures such as the Bible, Providence, or retribution in the afterlife. He did state that "the goodness, the justice, and the mercy of God are manifested in His works", but also that "the universe is governed by strict and immutable laws", which determine "small matters", such as who dies in a pestilence. At other times, he wrote or spoke in ways that contradicted a strict deist view, for example, plainly professing a belief in Providence. In some later writings in the 1890s, he was less optimistic about the goodness of God, observing that "if our Maker is all-powerful for good or evil, He is not in His right mind". At other times, he conjectured sardonically that perhaps God had created the world with all its tortures for some purpose of His own, but was otherwise indifferent to humanity, which was too petty and insignificant to deserve His attention anyway.

In 1901, Twain criticized the actions of the missionary Dr. William Scott Ament (1851–1909) because Ament and other missionaries had collected indemnities from Chinese subjects in the aftermath of the Boxer Uprising of 1900. Twain's response to hearing of Ament's methods was published in the North American Review in February 1901: To the Person Sitting in Darkness, and deals with examples of imperialism in China, South Africa, and with the U.S. occupation of the Philippines. A subsequent article, "To My Missionary Critics" published in The North American Review in April 1901, unapologetically continues his attack, but with the focus shifted from Ament to his missionary superiors, the American Board of Commissioners for Foreign Missions.

After his death, Twain's family suppressed some of his work that was especially irreverent toward conventional religion, including Letters from the Earth, which was not published until his daughter Clara reversed her position in 1962 in response to Soviet propaganda about the withholding. The anti-religious The Mysterious Stranger was published in 1916. Little Bessie, a story ridiculing Christianity, was first published in the 1972 collection Mark Twain's Fables of Man.

He raised money to build a Presbyterian Church in Nevada in 1864.

Twain created a reverent portrayal of Joan of Arc, a subject over which he had obsessed for forty years, studied for a dozen years and spent two years writing about. In 1900 and again in 1908 he stated, "I like Joan of Arc best of all my books, it is the best".

Those who knew Twain well late in life recount that he dwelt on the subject of the afterlife, his daughter Clara saying: "Sometimes he believed death ended everything, but most of the time he felt sure of a life beyond."

Twain's frankest views on religion appeared in his final work Autobiography of Mark Twain, the publication of which started in November 2010, 100 years after his death. In it, he said:

There is one notable thing about our Christianity: bad, bloody, merciless, money-grabbing, and predatory as it is – in our country particularly and in all other Christian countries in a somewhat modified degree – it is still a hundred times better than the Christianity of the Bible, with its prodigious crime – the invention of Hell. Measured by our Christianity of to-day, bad as it is, hypocritical as it is, empty and hollow as it is, neither the Deity nor his Son is a Christian, nor qualified for that moderately high place. Ours is a terrible religion. The fleets of the world could swim in spacious comfort in the innocent blood it has spilled.

Twain was a Freemason. He belonged to Polar Star Lodge No. 79 A.F.&A.M., based in St. Louis. He was initiated an Entered Apprentice on May 22, 1861, passed to the degree of Fellow Craft on June 12, and raised to the degree of Master Mason on July 10.

Twain visited Salt Lake City for two days and met there members of The Church of Jesus Christ of Latter-day Saints. They also gave him a Book of Mormon. He later wrote in Roughing It about that book:

The book seems to be merely a prosy detail of imaginary history, with the Old Testament for a model; followed by a tedious plagiarism of the New Testament.

Vivisection

Twain was opposed to the vivisection practices of his day. His objection was not on a scientific basis but rather an ethical one. He specifically cited the pain caused to the animal as his basis of his opposition:

I am not interested to know whether Vivisection produces results that are profitable to the human race or doesn't. ... The pains which it inflicts upon unconsenting animals is the basis of my enmity towards it, and it is to me sufficient justification of the enmity without looking further.

Pen names

Twain used different pen names before deciding on "Mark Twain". He signed humorous and imaginative sketches as "Josh" until 1863. Additionally, he used the pen name "Thomas Jefferson Snodgrass" for a series of humorous letters.

He maintained that his primary pen name came from his years working on Mississippi riverboats, where two fathoms, a depth indicating water safe for the passage of boat, was a measure on the sounding line. Twain is an archaic term for "two", as in "The veil of the temple was rent in twain." The riverboatman's cry was "mark twain" or, more fully, "by the mark twain", meaning "according to the mark [on the line], [the depth is] two [fathoms]", that is, "The water is 12 feet (3.7 m) deep and it is safe to pass."

Twain said that his famous pen name was not entirely his invention. In Life on the Mississippi, he wrote:

Captain Isaiah Sellers was not of literary turn or capacity, but he used to jot down brief paragraphs of plain practical information about the river, and sign them "MARK TWAIN", and give them to the New Orleans Picayune. They related to the stage and condition of the river, and were accurate and valuable; ... At the time that the telegraph brought the news of his death, I was on the Pacific coast. I was a fresh new journalist, and needed a nom de guerre; so I confiscated the ancient mariner's discarded one, and have done my best to make it remain what it was in his hands – a sign and symbol and warrant that whatever is found in its company may be gambled on as being the petrified truth; how I have succeeded, it would not be modest in me to say.

Twain's story about his pen name has been questioned by some with the suggestion that "mark twain" refers to a running bar tab that Twain would regularly incur while drinking at John Piper's saloon in Virginia City, Nevada. Samuel Clemens himself responded to this suggestion by saying, "Mark Twain was the nom de plume of one Captain Isaiah Sellers, who used to write river news over it for the New Orleans Picayune. He died in 1869 and as he could no longer need that signature, I laid violent hands upon it without asking permission of the proprietor's remains. That is the history of the nom de plume I bear."

In his autobiography, Twain writes further of Captain Sellers' use of "Mark Twain":

I was a cub pilot on the Mississippi River then, and one day I wrote a rude and crude satire which was leveled at Captain Isaiah Sellers, the oldest steamboat pilot on the Mississippi River, and the most respected, esteemed, and revered. For many years he had occasionally written brief paragraphs concerning the river and the changes which it had undergone under his observation during fifty years, and had signed these paragraphs "Mark Twain" and published them in the St. Louis and New Orleans journals. In my satire I made rude game of his reminiscences. It was a shabby poor performance, but I didn't know it, and the pilots didn't know it. The pilots thought it was brilliant. They were jealous of Sellers, because when the gray-heads among them pleased their vanity by detailing in the hearing of the younger craftsmen marvels which they had seen in the long ago on the river, Sellers was always likely to step in at the psychological moment and snuff them out with wonders of his own which made their small marvels look pale and sick. However, I have told all about this in "Old Times on the Mississippi." The pilots handed my extravagant satire to a river reporter, and it was published in the New Orleans True Delta. That poor old Captain Sellers was deeply wounded. He had never been held up to ridicule before; he was sensitive, and he never got over the hurt which I had wantonly and stupidly inflicted upon his dignity. I was proud of my performance for a while, and considered it quite wonderful, but I have changed my opinion of it long ago. Sellers never published another paragraph nor ever used his nom de guerre again.

Legacy and depictions

Trademark white suit

While Twain is often depicted wearing a white suit, modern representations suggesting that he wore them throughout his life are unfounded. Evidence suggests that Twain began wearing white suits on the lecture circuit, after the death of his wife Olivia ("Livy") in 1904. However, there is also evidence showing him wearing a white suit before 1904. In 1882, he sent a photograph of himself in a white suit to 18-year-old Edward W. Bok, later publisher of the Ladies Home Journal, with a handwritten dated note. The white suit did eventually become his trademark, as illustrated in anecdotes about this eccentricity (such as the time he wore a white summer suit to a Congressional hearing during the winter). McMasters' The Mark Twain Encyclopedia states that Twain did not wear a white suit in his last three years, except at one banquet speech.

In his autobiography, Twain writes of his early experiments with wearing white out-of-season:

Next after fine colors, I like plain white. One of my sorrows, when the summer ends, is that I must put off my cheery and comfortable white clothes and enter for the winter into the depressing captivity of the shapeless and degrading black ones. It is mid-October now, and the weather is growing cold up here in the New Hampshire hills, but it will not succeed in freezing me out of these white garments, for here the neighbors are few, and it is only of crowds that I am afraid. (Source: Wikipedia)

Lightning Source UK Ltd.
Milton Keynes UK
UKHW011836200520
363522UK00001B/110

9 789353 855468